BIRDS

of the

Yorkshire Dales

Grey Heron

By the same author:

A FEW MILLION BIRDS

BIRDWATCH ROUND SCOTLAND

HIGHLAND SPRING

WEST HIGHLAND SUMMER

HIGHLAND AUTUMN

HIGHLAND WINTER

A YEAR WITH THE CURLEWS

PENNINE BIRDS (with Bill Robson)

LAKELAND BIRDS (with Bill Robson)

BIRD-WATCHING IN YORKSHIRE (with Bob Dickens)

A PASSION FOR PUFFINS (illustrated by David Binns)

BIRDS

of the

Yorkshire Dales

by

W R Mitchell

MBE, Hon D.Litt.

Illustrated

by

David Binns

Birds have a way of making their own rules to fit circumstances which may not be entirely clear to human beings. All one can do is to state the facts as one sees them.

Ralph Chislett (1946)

CASTLEBERG

1998

For
DAN BINNS
An artist who loved the dale-country

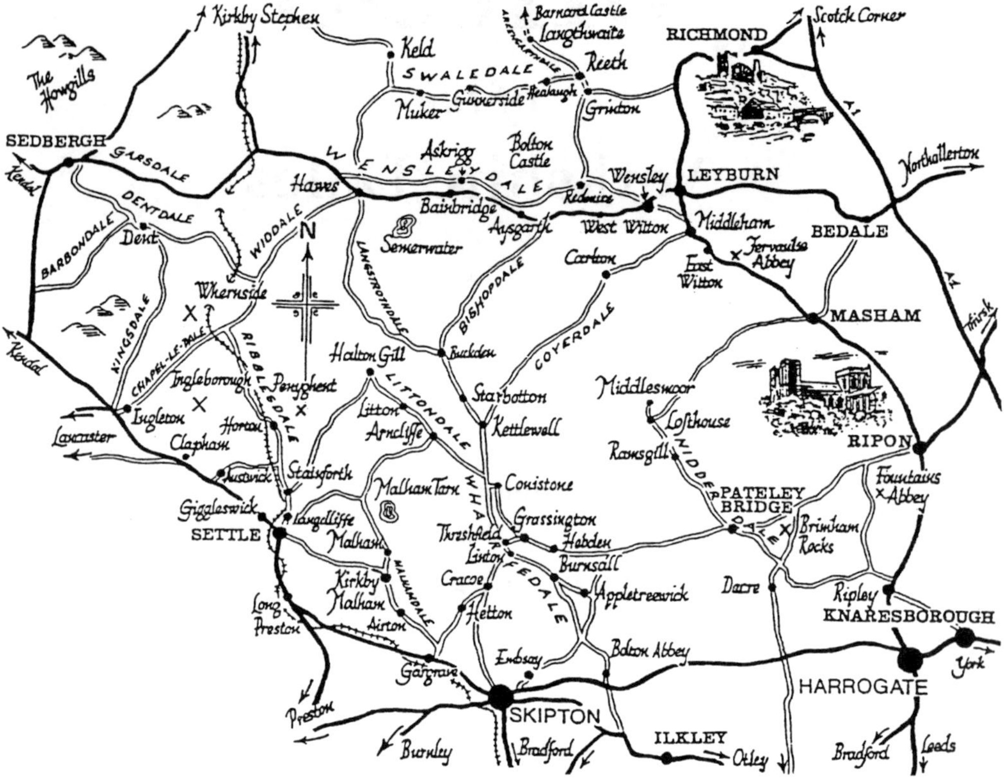

A **Castleberg** Book.
First published in the United Kingdom in 1998.

ISBN 1 871064 77 5
Typeset in Palatino, printed and bound in the United Kingdom by Lamberts Print & Design, Station Road, Settle, North Yorkshire, BD24 9AA.
Published by Castleberg, 18 Yealand Avenue, Giggleswick, Settle, North Yorkshire, BD24 0AY.

Contents

Curlews

Foreword

by Rob Hume

Editor, BIRDS, the
RSPB magazine

Meadow Pipit

A glance at the list of books "by the same author" in the front of any book is revealing. Bill Mitchell's titles show a prediliction for wild places: Scotland and Yorkshire, hills and lakes, rocky coastlines and their particular birds. Many of the birds seem to be instilled with much the same qualities as the landscapes they inhabit: the tough, belligerent ring ouzel on its frost-shattered crag, the richly-coloured red grouse crouched deep within leggy heather, the coal-black, hardy raven flying from its big stick nest beneath an overhang of dark rock.

There are exquisite moments with the birds of these habitats, too, like the first ecstatic bubbling notes of a curlew's song, the delicacy of a cock whinchat, so pale against the dark heather or the rich colours of a drake teal on the black water of a peaty pool. Many such moments are captured by the fine work of David Binns as well as Bill Mitchell's words in this book.

A look at the contents page reveals more. Bill Mitchell is interested in people, too, and the places where they love and have left their mark: inevitable, I suppose, in the Yorkshire Dales. Not much is left that has not been shaped by people in one way or another: the moorland itself, the marginal land, the woods and parks. The villages, the scattering of old stone barns, the abundance of drystone walls, all add immensely to the Dales landscapes and enrich them and the wildlife in their way.

Yet now it so often seems that human influence is becoming less welcome, less positive. One important role this book can play is simply to instil a respect for the wildlife that will help to ensure it survives the coming decades. Through reading it, more people may come to love the Yorkshire Dales and their birds, if only from a distance, and that is surely a good thing.

A Lapwing and its chicks

INTRODUCTION

Bird-watching has become a major leisuretime occupation. The Royal Society for the Protection of Birds now has over one million members. Many of them are content to watch birds that appear to view on country walks. Others specialise in single species, two Dales examples being those of Peter Wright and Ian Appleyard.

Peter, who lives at Skipton, spent 25 years amassing information about the merlin, a ground-nesting falcon, at its nesting haunts on the Barden Moors above Wharfedale. Ian Appleyard, of Ripon, made a 15-year study of the ring ouzel, investigating the territories of 353 pairs.

A third category of bird-watcher is the "twitcher", a person of restless energy to whom birds are something to be sought, then ticked off on a list. Alerted to rarities by a sophisticated telephone information service, "twitchers" by the hundred converge on specific spots. When a red kite, which is a curiosity in the dale-country, gave an air display at Gouthwaite reservoir, in Nidderdale, in February, 1997, up to 200 bird-watchers followed the bird's every movement. They also saw a young golden eagle turn on its back in mid-air to fend off a buzzard with its talons.

Birds of the Yorkshire Dales is for those who love this region and its wildlife – and wish they knew a little more. The book also takes a realistic attitude towards bird identification in the wild, concentrating on form, manner and calls rather than fine points of plumage. Little information is provided about eggs. A bird-watcher should be content to watch birds from a distance.

With few exceptions, wild birds and their nests have legal protection. The aforementioned Peter Wright had a special licence to study merlins and to handle chicks, which he weighed regularly as part of the process of monitoring the general health of the birds. On one occasion, he was checking some new hatchlings when he noticed there was something wrong with a foot of one of the chicks. Some of its toes were fused together. A trip to a vet and some laser treatment was arranged. The chick was safely returned.

Until quite recent times, birdwatchers were few in number and well spread. Parsons and teachers were among those who watched birds and wrote about them. Yet a century and more ago, there was a strong natural history movement among working class folk in industrial towns on either side of the Pennines who visited the Dales with naturalist societies or by rail, bike or Shank's pony to follow up their interests. Chris Cheetham was one of them. He eventually settled at Austwick, served for many years as secretary of the Yorkshire Naturalists' Union, cycled everywhere, knew his birds – and had a species of daddy-longlegs named after him.

When I began to study Pennine birds, with a special interest in those nesting on crags, bird-watchers were thinly scattered and James Fisher was claiming to be the only professional ornithologist in the land. The devotees I met were a bunch of cheerful amateurs who set out with heavy binoculars and even heavier plate-cameras and tripods to track down and record the nesting activity of a wide range of birds. When I joined the RSPB some 50 years ago, I could not have foreseen that the cosy little society would grow into such a vast organisation, at the sharp-end of conservation and linked with like-minded people and bodies the world over.

The area covered by this book is the Yorkshire Dales National Park, plus the upper valleys of the Hodder (west) and Nidd (east). It is a delectable region, about 20 per cent of which is officially classified as being of special scientific interest. Birds do not exist in a vacuum. They perform their annual rituals against a backdrop of calluna moorland, in bluebell woods, on limestone grassland speckled with flowers of pastel shades, and in floriferous upland hay meadows, where a dazzling array of summer colour is sustained by up to 80 different plant species.

The sides of rivers and becks have their distinctive bird species like the dipper, grey wagtail and sandpiper. They also form part of a rich Dales lore. In her delightful booklet *A Bonny Hubbleshoo,* which in Dales talk means "a complete jumble", Dr Margaret Batty has a section on vernacular names. She mentions some Swaledale terms for birds, such as blackoozle for blackbird, bullspink for bullfinch, crake for a crow, jinnyoolet for owl, moorgam for grouse and moorpoot for young grouse. A lapwing was known as a pee-wit, locally teeafit. Vernacular names for birds might vary from dale to dale. Thomas H Nelson, in his two-volume *The Birds of Yorkshire,* published in 1907, had a most varied collection from different areas of a vast county. Examples from the Craven district of the west are whinchacker (whinchat), midden daup (carrion crow) and pit martin (sand martin).

My old friend Tom Hey, a Dales lad who became a journalist in London, was fond of recalling piefinch for chaffinch, Peggy dishwater for the pied wagtail and titlark for the meadow pipit. The whitethroat had the most apt name of nettle-creeper and the great tit was saw-whet, from its call, which sounds like a rusty saw in operation. The Dales name shepster, for the starling, is presumably from sheep-stare. The association between bird and beast is close. A starling, perching on the back of a sheep, collects tit-bits of food or some wool for its nest.

The information given in *Birds of the Yorkshire Dales* is in a popular rather than academic form. An attempt has been made to group distinctive birds according to the type of landscape in which they might be seen. This should not be interpreted too strictly. Landform and climate govern birds; they do not acknowledge man-made boundaries.

For example, the wren is found almost everywhere. I see it regularly on my morning walk and in spring it utters a cascade of sharp notes, quite often using a fencing post as a perch, and eyeing me from a range of a few yards. Another time, when I sat beside a a pothole on an austere fell, a wren appeared to feed in a mossy, area near where a beck was pouring into an open shaft. Ring ouzels have been known to nest inside potholes. A pair of dippers, of a species usually associated with rivers, made a mossy nest on a ledge in Gaping Gill, the natural shaft on Ingleborough into which Fell Beck tumbles as a waterfall over twice the height of Niagara.

In a study of wildlife, it's the unexpected that enthrals. It might be the sighting of an uncommon hill bird with the curious name of twite – one of the "little brown jobs" but with a stout yellow beak. It might be an unexpectedly close view of a lapwing – say from a car, while travelling on a moorland road. This relatively common bird is not just green and white. Its back and wings are shot over with a greenish-purple gloss. If the lapwing was rare, hundreds of people would travel to the Dales specifically to see it. An angry *caw* from high up might be some testy carrion crow defending its air space. Perhaps the bird is hustling a short-eared owl, a buzzard or even a peregrine falcon.

An imaginative approach to ornithology was demonstrated by a friend who on a spring day was walking along the edge of a beck when he found the ransacked nest of a pair of long-tailed tits in the fork of a big elder bush. Astonishingly, this type of nest is elasticated. As the young grow, the nest grows with them. The nest was taken home, spread on a table, and a study made of the variety of bird feathers used in its construction out of a total of up to 2,000. The extremely small feathers included partridge, tawny owl, wood pigeon, carrion crow, cock and hen pheasant and woodcock.

With research advancing on a wide front, we have a deep insight into the lives of birds and natural processes. For example, the nightjar, a summer bird visitor which in the Dales is near the northern edge of its range, was known as the gabble-ratchet in Nidderdale. It still nests in the vicinity of Brimham Rocks. The bird was thought to embody the soul of an unbaptised infant, doomed to wander forever through the air. When not active, the nightjar lies on the ground, where its plumage tones in with dead vegetation. Field research suggests that nightjars, which dart and wheel in their quest for night-flying moths and beetles, are in effect moonbirds. They time their activities – mating, laying eggs, and feeding their young – to the occurrence of a full moon.

By no means everything about birds is recorded in books. A bird photographer at a long-tailed tit nest noticed a curious aspect of the removal of the faecal sac, containing waste products from the nestlings. Because the young are massed with their heads out of the hole, the one depositing a faecal sac clings upside down on the ceiling of the nest and puts its tail over the heads of its companions. So it does not soil them.

A bird-watcher tends to revere a bird in which he or she is specially interested. I have a fondness for the dipper, which I see most days on my early morning round in North Ribblesdale. The podgy little bird with dark plumage and a white bib feeds by turning stones on the bed of the stream and snaffling anything edible that is thus exposed.

Bird-watching never loses its savour because it is changeful. Some species decline in number while others, reacting to changing conditions, extend their nesting range. A good example is the oystercatcher. This black and white bird with a long red bill which during the nesting season flies with noisy calls over shingle beds beside the Skirfare or across a reservoir like Grimwith, between Hebden and Greenhow Hill, is a coastal bird that began nesting in the upper Dales in the 1960s. Another bird of the beach, which has its emissaries in the Dales, is the ringed plover, here at the southern end of its huge range. This dainty little plover nests on a beach made for it at Grimwith reservoir, in a valley approached from the road from Grassington to Greenhow. The spread of the collared dove from the Mediterranean through Europe and, from about 1957 through Britain, is nothing less than astonishing.

Under the Countryside Act of 1981, it is an offence to kill, injure or take any wild bird or damage its nest or take its eggs, except for certain pest and sporting species. In addition to this basic protection, it is an offence to intentionally disturb certain specially protected birds while they are nesting or rearing young, including peregrine, merlin, goshawk, hen harrier and kingfisher.

Those who find special interest in rare and unusual birds may obtain information about them from Birdline North East on 01426 983963 or Birdline North West on 0151 336 6188. For information, ring these premium rate lines: 0891 700246 (North East); 0891 700249 (North West).

Aids to Bird-watching

Buy a set of OS maps of the Dales. The Outdoor Leisure series at 2½ inch/4cm to the mile will cost about £10. The maps have been specially designed to serve a popular recreation area. Carry a notebook and writing materials so you keep a record of your observations and, if in doubt, can make a rough sketch of a bird, highlighting features to be checked at leisure against a book description.

If you plan a walk into hill country, take some waterproof clothing. At high elevation, the weather is fickle. A sunny day might quickly change into one that is wet and windy. Avoid garish colours. Wear some comfortable boots.

Choose a good pair of binoculars, so that with care it will last your lifetime. If in doubt, consult a specialist dealer. Avoid being tempted by binoculars that are impressively large. At a cost of about £100, choose a magnification of between 7 and 10. Ensure they give a reasonably large image, can be focussed on objects near at hand as well as afar and are light enough to be held without undue fatigue.

A good general handbook, such as the recently published *Guide to*

British Birds, by Dominic Couzens (Collins, £12.99), will supplement my book on Dales bird life. In the general guide, a mass of information is succinctly and tidily presented. Anyone unfamiliar with bird calls, especially those of the large warbler family and other aforementioned "little brown jobs", might invest in birds sounds presented on tape or cassette. There's no real substitute for listening to birds out-of-doors, then patiently identifying the songsters.

The Fieldfare: a winter visitor to the Dales

Meadow Pipit

DALE COUNTRY

The region known as the Yorkshire Dales is spacious and uncomplicated. Two-thirds of the Dales National Park consist of moors and fells, the last named being derived from *fjell,* a name of Norse origin. It was the Norse settlers of the 9th and 10th centuries who bestowed their name *dalr* for a valley, hence the word "dale".

Dale-country is a landscape of horizontals – of bare ridges rather than upsweeping peaks. Rarely will you have to tilt your head upwards to take in the scenery, as at the heart of the Lake District. In Wensleydale, some ridges and terraces look so neat someone using a giant ruler might have laid them out.

The geology of the Yorkshire Dales is complex but can be easily explained to the non-specialist by reference to a sandwich cake with various layers, though lacking a cream filling! Rocks of the Carboniferous age, laid down as sediments in the sea, were raised, bringing into existence an elevated plateau, tilting slightly towards the east. The dales are, in a basic sense, the drainage system.

Compare the V profile of a water-carved gill with the U shape of a typical dale. During what is popularly known as the Ice Age – it lasted, with temperate interludes, for a million years – glaciers deepened and smoothed the sides of the old river valleys, plastering the sides with mush we call "boulder clay". With water draining mainly towards the east, the major rivers of the Yorkshire Dales have long and fairly languid courses. Swale, Ure, Wharfe and Nidd flow into the Ouse, thence to the Humber and the North Sea. The Aire, having taken a southward course through Malhamdale, eventually flows eastwards through what is known as the Aire Gap. The western watercourses, Rawthey and Ribble, initially have short, sharp courses and the water enters the Irish Sea.

Silurian. An area of ancient slates occurs as the Howgill Fells which, though now part of Cumbria, remain in the Yorkshire Dales National Park. The Dent Fault, a crack in the earth's crust, separates the rounded domes of the Howgills from the ridges and plateaux of the dale-country.

Limestone. The bed of limestone which is seen most clearly in the south-western part of the Yorkshire Dales National Park was laid down in a clear tropical sea about 300 million years ago. Limestone country has dramatic features like "pavements", scars, dry valleys and an extensive system of potholes [open shafts] and caves.

Limestone lights up the landscape and has the chameleon ability to adjust its tones to that of the prevailing conditions. In stormy weather, it is livid; and when the conditions are "cloudy bright" it has a delicate pearl-grey hue. On a spring evening after stormy conditions, the scars gleams white as chalk against a blue-grey sky. Erosion has led to the presence of "pavements", consisting of clints [level pieces of rock] and grykes [deep crevices], such as you will find in Chapel-le-Dale or across the top of Malham Cove.

Yoredale Series. Yoredale is an old word for Wensleydale, in which valley are some of the best exposures of this series of rocks which lie above the limestone and rise about 1,000ft/305m in alternating bands of slate, grit and limestone. Laid down as marine sediments and forming an attractive "rhythmic succession", the Yoredales are seen to great advantage when viewing the Three Peaks – Whernside, Ingleborough and Penyghent.

The beds of limestone, standing proud along the sides of the dales, notably Wensleydale and Upper Wharfedale, are conspicuous terraces. This type of country has some impressive waterfalls, notably Hardraw Force, where a beck falls from the lip of a 90ft/27m scar. This splendid feature might be visited for a small charge.

Millstone Grit. Capping the big hills to the west, and overlying vast stretches of landscape to the east, is millstone grit. Being impervious to water, this gritstone enables them to keep their shapes. The rock is so named because being coarse it made excellent millstones which did not over-heat the grain.

Ice Age. Much of what we see today was sculpted during the Ice Age. At least three glaciations occurred in a million-year-old spectacular, the third glaciation reaching a peak 25,000 years ago. We are probably living in an inter-glacial and the ice-sheets will return in due course.

Landscape. The dale-country is a farmed landscape and no true wilderness remains. Even the uplands have been taken in hand within a gridiron pattern of drystone walls, many of them dating to the Enclosure Awards of the 18th and 19th centuries. The region has been for centuries a huge sheep range.

Within the Dales area are diverse landforms - high fells, crags, heather moors, rough pastures and meadows. In the moorland plant mix are ling, bilberry, cowberry, cloudberry – food for moorland birds, especially the red grouse. The Dales have their "honeypots", such as Aysgarth Falls, Malham and Bolton Abbey.

Wensleydale and Wharfedale attract thousands of day-trippers. Parts of Swaledale do not seem to have changed for half a century and more. At Low Row, a section of the main road has jay-walking cows, being part of the common pasture.

The Climate. The Pennines form a considerable barrier against the storms sweeping in from the west. From the north-east comes the snow that sticks, even squeaks. In 1947, the worst winter in human memory, the road from the head of Swaledale to Mallerstang was blocked for 13 weeks. The thaw comes in two stages, the first being the dispersal of snow from lower land. A beck that has tinkled between white banks acquires a deeper voice as the water level rises. Then a day or two later, the fell-country snow capitulates. "Snaw broth" descends by a thousand runnels bearing patches of brown froth from the peat.

In late March, when there's still a dab of snow high on Ingleborough, daffodils are blooming in the villages. Bird life responds to the longer periods of daylight and goes into the breeding mode.

Wet and windy showers in April are known as "lamb storms" and in May as "gosling storms". May's climatic vagaries include the "cowquake", a cold snap occurring as cows are turned out for grazing after being confined to the shippons for months.

High Hills. A dalesman remarked on the "terrible amount of unseen grund 'at lies between t'dales." On the highest ground, the most widespread bird is the meadow pipit, which returns to the nesting area in mid-March, not long after the skylark, which is becoming uncommon. On ridges where vegetation is sparse, golden plover in nuptial dress, their backs peppered with gold and with dark underparts, circle with doleful calls. On moorland, where ling and associated shrubby plants have rooted in peat, the cock grouse utters its gutteral calls as he claims a prime territory in November and, by March, is defending it against other cock birds with such vigour that feathers fly.

At the fringes of high ground, where rush-bobs abound, cock lapwings, dark green and white, with conspicuous head tufts, give an exhuberant call – *oo-ip* – as they twist and tumble, beating their tufty wings so vigorously that a deep throbbing sound is heard. In grandfather's time, tewits were so common it was possible to fill a cap with eggs and still leave plenty to be hatched out naturally.

A snipe "bleats" when, during a brief dive, at the edge o' dark, as dusk was known to the old-time dalesfolk, air is forced through the stiff barbs of the outer feathers of the tail. Between late March and August, the wheatear – named after the prominent white patch at the rump - occupies many bare stony heights. The ring ouzel, our "mountain blackbird", returns to the Dales at about the same time and frequents stony country, such as scree slopes and steep-sided narrow gills.

Standing Water. The only natural lakes are Semerwater and Malham Tarn but reservoirs abound and act as staging posts for migrants passing from coast to coast. The upper valley of the Nidd, including Gouthwaite, a compensation reservoir in an area where there was a post-glacial lake, has become the premier site in Yorkshire for observing birds of prey in the off-season. In February, 1997, eight different species of raptor were viewed. They were a golden eagle, two red kites, five hen harriers, twenty common buzzards, a merlin, and a peregrine, a sparrow hawk and kestrel.

At Chelker, beside the A59 between Skipton and Ilkley, a wise motorist keeps his eye on the roads. A passenger, looking at the reservoir, sees a great-crested grebe in its springtime finery or a coot, a white patch on its head contrasting with the funearal black of the rest of its plumage. Early in 1988, a black-necked grebe entertained watchers on Gallaber, now more frequently called Hellifield Flashes.

Red kites observed around Leighton Reservoir, between Lofthouse and Masham, are almost certainly from stock introduced into three new areas - the Chilterns, the Midlands and Scotland. Gouthwaite reservoir in Nidderdale is the prime bird-watching area, especially in winter. No less than 16 common buzzards were recorded in mid-December, 1997.

Meadow and Pasture. The Dales, like many another pastoral area, is a green landscape but the wall-to-wall grass on the best ground is a ryegrass mix, planted to ensure an early flush for the farm stock. It is taken green as silage, and there are usually one or more cuts a year. This response to the need for greater production – a modern fad – has gravely affected the wildlife of the Dales. The emerald greenness of the modern landscape has replaced, in most cases, the old-fashioned hay meadow, with its dazzling array of colour in June as eighty or more plants are flowering.

Haytime was in July, by which time the flowers had set seed and birds like the corncrake and curlew had ensured the continuance of their kind. In areas which resounded each spring to the calls of tewit, curlew and redshank there is now an unaccustomed springtime hush. Once the dalesfolk had their sleep pattern disturbed by that prize skulker, the corncrake, which utters a repetitive *crex, crex.*

Woodland. The clearance of woodland began several thousand years ago and today just one per cent of the Dales landscape bears semi-natural broad-leaved woodland, much of it in the form of ash woods, such as might be seen on the sides of upper Wharfedale. A few areas of original ancient woodland and shrub cover hold stunted ash, hazel, hawthorn and bird cherry. Such a tract of woodland provides food and shelter for the redstart, willow warbler and woodcock.

Other tracts of old woodland are found in the water-carved tributary valleys known as gills, which were difficult to farm. In many old woods, the trees and rocks become lagged with moss. A particularly good example is at Janet's Foss, Malhamdale, where aged trees have been left where they fell, providing accommodation for a variety of insects – and consequently food for birds.

Ash, rowan, birch, sessile oak, alder and willow are being planted across 82 acres of moorland at Blea Gill, near Grimwith Reservoir, and also near Hawes in Wensleydale and Keld in Swaledale specifically to help black grouse re-establish themselves. It is hoped that the few surviving black grouse will use new woodland to re-establish themselves in the Dales.

Hanging woods are the summer resorts of redstart, pied flycatcher, green woodpecker and wood warbler. At low elevations, as in Bolton Woods, by the mid-Wharfe, the mature stands of timber are good for warblers, also pied and spotted flycatchers, nuthatch and great spotted woodpecker. The redstart prefers open woodland conditions, such as high-lying ash woods and the species may also be found nesting in drystone walls.

Blocks of sitka spruce muffle sounds from the busy outside world. There is the stillness normally associated with large churches. In the stillness, the alarm calls of blue tit sounds like a pneumatic drill. The thin calls of a goldcrest have been compared with a fairy's sewing machine. Nesting in the areas of larch within the conifer forests, which smother areas of the upper dales, is the sparrow hawk, a woodland fiend. When it has young to feed it establishes plucking areas which become strewn with feathers of many species. The big twiggy nest takes on the appearance of a butcher's shop.

WINGS OVER THE DALES

The Snowy Owl

The latest phase of glaciation in the Yorkshire Dales was at its height 25,000 years ago, when the landscape was ice-locked, with just the tops of the highest hills in view. Another 15,000 years or so elapsed before the land, clear of its crushing burden of ice, was able to support life in the form of plants, mammals and birds. For unnumbered years, the area, with its hills, ridges, valleys, glacial lakes and thundering water-courses had the austere appearance of the Arctic region today.

Among the birds suited to life in the freezer were snowy owls, silent hunters, like big white moths, and ptarmigan, birds for all seasons, moulting thrice a year to suit the changing tones on mountain tops. I would imagine that the dotterel, a bird of high plateaux, would find the conditions favourable during a visit to nest in a chilling summer. The greenshank would be at home eventually between the tree-line and tundra.

When the climate ameliorated the ice-cap melted and the blue snouts of glaciers fell back, the old river valleys had been scoured and deepened. Everywhere was the gleam of water where moraines provided natural dams. Moss and lichen, then assemblages of plants, began to clothe the rocks and boulder-clay. The first trees would be dwarf versions of willow and juniper, which put down long roots and keep their heads down. The trilling song of the snow bunting, with a nest among the jumbled rocks of a scree, would infuse life into the wilderness.

At some indefinable period, a variant of the widely-distributed willow grouse ceased to go white in winter and became the so-called red grouse, retaining a reddish hue the whole year round, though retaining white feathering on legs and feet. The gruff voice of the raven and the eerie wail of the red-throated diver would carry far across the austere northern landscape. The greylag, ancestor of our domestic goose, nesting in the wetlands, would doubtless be there, leading its goslings on to the nearest lake for safety and to dine on insect food.

Woodland Cover

Silver birch, its roots locking together the gravel beds, provided a stable base for the formation of soil and attacted nesting birds - redpoll, brambling, fieldfare and redwing. The open nature of woodland and the ragged vegetation would suit the black grouse. Where pine was established, the capercaillie, a monster of the woods, serenaded the demure females, which are now known as greyhens, with a medley of short, sharp notes climaxed with a "pop" and a gurgle. The bones of capercaillie have been found in caves in the dale-country, including upper Swaledale.

In Mesolithic times, judging by remains found in middens, the fauna included crane, merganser, great-crested grebe, dabchick and lapwing.

Deciduous trees such as oak and lime gradually replaced the pines. Conditions in the wildwood were right for the goshawk, a fierce hunter which flew with the power of short, blunt wings. Two other typical woodland birds of these northern parts were robin and dunnock.

Britain became an island some 6,000 years ago. The coming of man gradually upset the natural balance. For centuries, through slash-and-burn or by using a heavy implement like a stone axe, early settlers desecrated the woodland. Domestic stock, by their grazing and browsing, ensured there would be little or no natural regeneration of the settled areas. The greylag goose and the mallard were probably domesticated during the Iron Age, through a process of imprinting, whereby the young follow whatever creature their eyes settle on after hatching.

With more open conditions, the kestrel could spread from those tracts of rocky ground to which its ancestors had been restricted by the onset of woodland. The open hills were appealing to hen harrier and merlin but there was still shrub-cover for nesting blackbirds. A Celtic poet wrote of the bird's "joyous note when he claps his wings". The cuckoo, heralding the spring, led another Celtic poet to write of "the cooing of the cuckoo from the tree on the brink of summer."

Norsemen and Normans

The raven, sacred to the Norsefolk who colonised the upper dale-country in the 9th and 10th centuries, walked fearlessly through their settlements. Old men would tell of two ravens that were owned by Odin, god of war. These clever birds, which he called Hugin and Munin, meaning Thought and Memory, flew over the world by day and each evening related what they had seen to the Raven God, one of the names by which Odin was known. Some of the traditional nesting haunts of the raven were incorporated in Norse placenames, such as

Ravenseat, at the head of Swaledale, Ravenscar near Great Whernside and Raven's Gill, in Nidderdale.

When the Normans held the country in a firm grip, the dale-country was divided among several of William the Conqueror's favourite knights. The wild upper dales remained so, being mainly forest, though this name is derived from *foris,* meaning land set apart for hunting. Such an area, having its own game laws, was in effect a nature reserve. Eagles and buzzards were common. Where there was open ground, merlins snatched small birds and fed the corpses to their downy young at a nest among the heather. The village of Arncliffe, in Littondale, is said to have been named after the erne or sea eagle, which nested on one of the mighty limestone crags and, being huge, has been compared by a modern ornithologist to "a flying barn door".

Peregrines taken from eyries on the crags as well-grown young were trained for falconry, which was not just a sport; it became a means of providing fresh food for the larder. Falconry came to England with the returning Crusaders of the 10th and 1lth centuries. Certain species of bird were allocated to a hierarchy, reflecting their social positions. The peregrine was reserved for the top end of the social scale, the merlin was a lady's hawk and the kestrel the species kept by a sporting priest. He needed patience and limitless faith to make anything of such an individualistic creature.

Birds for the Table

A medieval banquet included several mute swans. When Landseer, a favourite artist of Queen Victoria, was commissioned by the Duke of Devonshire to provide a painting of Bolton Priory, he made sketches locally then painted a monastic interior which was not distinctively Bolton, the Prior being shown as he received dues in kind from tenants. The birds included a swan. The Duke did not care much for the picture, having expected the artist to provide a study of the Priory in its fine setting. Landseer's painting was exhibited at the Royal Academy in 1834 and now has a place of honour in the entrance hall of Chatsworth, the Derbyshire home of the Devonshires. From the 13th to the 18th centuries, swans were counted as the property of the Crown and were assigned to others by special license.

The accounts of Skipton Castle (1604-1639) reveal that the Clifford family had developed a taste for grouse, possibly taken from moorland above Wharfedale, where the family were major landowners. In 1784, Marmaduke Tunstall wrote about red cock [red grouse], a fine species which, like the black grouse, "has been much diminished these late years to my knowledge." He blamed in part the Enclosure Acts under which a considerable amount of what had been common land was allocated to individuals who had, by the terms of the Act, to enclose it. This was done in the dale-country by rearing drystone walls, which soon formed a futuristic pattern on the landscape.

The introduction of firearms was, to the landowners, a chance to shoot specific wild birds for fun. With a decline in falconry, the peregrine lost its protection. In the 18th century, ravens vanished from their urban haunts and survived on a few remote crags. The birds were now classified as vermin, and the churchwardens offered a bounty for everyone that was killed. Though basically a carrion-eater, and thus helping to clean up the countryside, the raven was accused of attacking sheep. In most cases its pick-axe beak broke through the ribs of a corpse so the bird could reach the rank flesh.

The churchwardens' accounts at Dent for 1713 reveal that 10d was distributed to those who brought eight raven heads. Four years later, the number of ravens slaughtered had risen to 35 and the disbursement was 5s.10d. Any creature edible to man featured in his larder. Rook pie was popular. The rook, also known as a crow, featured in a couplet chanted in the Craven district:

Crow, crow, get out of my sight,
Or else I'll eat thy liver and lights.

Mr Fothergill's Diary

The diary of Charles Fothergill for 1805 provides a valuable record of bird life in the Dales at the dawn of the 19th century. Fothergill had a tour in "the north-western dales". His family, well-known Quakers, had built Carr End by Semerwater. It was to this fine house that Charles (1782-1840), a somewhat profligate young man, returned when his efforts to achieve fame and fortune elsewhere had come to nothing. He was fascinated by folk lore and natural history, both of which feature prominently in his writings.

On a visit to Carr End, his uncle recounted the quaint story of wrens roosting in the nests of martins under the eaves of houses. This occurred during a cold snap in winter. Uncle had counted as many as nine wrens entering one martin nest. Among the fanciful notions accepted by Charles Fothergill was that the heron laid on fat at the time of the full moon and gradually became lean again as it declined. Charles confided in his journal: "If there is any truth in this notion, it must chiefly be owing to this birds being able to see to feed in the night when the moon shines and not at other times."

Charles was familiar with red grouse, or "grous" as he spelt the name. He noted that in severe winters, birds left the moors and were seen about the moor-edge hamlets, "frequently sitting on the chimney pots for warmth and sometimes falling down them…Not very long ago a grous absolutely took refuge in the town of Hawes from the intensity of cold." There were areas where birch trees grew from a tangle of vegetation. These places suited black grouse, which (wrote Charles) had once been common on the moors. He was still gratified to hear the clear whistling of golden plover. Taking a "wild and quick walk of 5 miles in the dusk of the evening over high moors to Richmond" he heard the birds pipe frequently.

At Middleham he saw a pair of tame ravens which "always roost with their faces towards the east". At Semerwater, kingfishers were reported to fly out over the lake "in the manner of the Fly catcher, hover awhile in the air, then suddenly plunge in the water to take their prey and return to their station: this they will do many times in succession." He reported on trigger-happy farmers, one of whom shot a peregrine falcon which had begun nesting at Hardraw Scar. A farmer in Raydale who lost a number of goslings unaccountably found the remains of them in the nest of a pair of barn owls and "ordered the family of owls to execution."

Then, as now, carrion crows did not miss a chance to have an easy meal. Among their prey were "foolish young geese". A pair of crows would gravely march up to a goose with goslings at foot. The old goose, in defence of her young, ran at the nearest crow; whereupon the other crow grabbed one or more of the goslings. "The two robbers immediately made off, leaving the poor goose a dupe to her ill judged valour."

There was merit, not condemnation, in countryfolk slaying hawks. As game-rearing interests developed in the 19th century, any bird with a hooked beak was shot as a predator. About the year 1871, an eagle was killed by one of the Duke of Devonshire's gamekeepers near Bolton Abbey and, stuffed and mounted, was sent for display to the Duke's principal home at Chatsworth.

Sporting Days

The vogue for shooting gamebirds evolved in the 19th century. Woodland which incorporated groves of rhododendrons provided cover for pheasants, descended from Asiatic fowls introduced to this country in Roman or Norman times. Two hundred "fessauntes" were among the items of food eaten at a banquet held at Cawood, by the lower Wharfe, in 1466. Gaudy cock pheasants, the ancestors of which had nested in reed-beds in marshy areas of China, were now classified as woodland birds and were good to eat. Thomas Allis (1844) wrote of its Yorkshire distribution: "As common as shooters and poachers will allow them to be." When the pheasant first appeared in upper Swaledale, the beauty of the cock bird entranced the dalesfolk. A number of cock birds were slain and "stuffed" to be displayed in glass cases.

At first, there were the "black-necks", then "ring-necks", reared in large numbers under broody hens purchased cheaply from local farms. Partridges nested in hedge-bottoms. On the bare hills, when the wind drew a comb through vast areas of heather, a small army of gamekeepers eliminated so-called vermin, mainly birds with hooked beaks. Grouse, unlike pheasants, lost their wild spirit and were useless for sport if they were hand-reared. The grouse, if left to themselves, would have regulated their own numbers, for the population is cyclical, rising and falling in spells of between six and seven years.

With the refinement of sport with pheasant and grouse, and its appeal to the new-rich of the industrial revolution, the gamekeeper became a skilled eliminator of any creature which so much as cast a covetous eye on a bird, its eggs or chicks. He had more trouble counteracting the efforts of poachers, who were known on warm, calm evenings, to light sticks of sulphur under trees where pheasants were roosting. They also made cones of paper, into which they poured treacle and some wheat, then secured the cones. The hungry pheasants soon had these attached to their heads and were vulnerable.

A gamekeeper did not receive much money but was content to have a secure job with free house, no rent or rates to pay, a garden to till and perhaps even a pig for the family larder. When on duty, he shot hawks and owls, also crows, stoats and weasels. Ralph Chislett, a notable Yorkshire ornithologist, did admit when considering the sad effect on the status of the larger hawks, "the privacy ensured to breeding grouse has helped such birds as the golden plover to survive in greater numbers."

In an extensive section on birds in *Studies in Nidderdale* by Joseph Lucas, 1867-1872, it was reported that "buzzards are occasionally seen on the moors". Subsequently, Lucas recorded the success of gamekeepers against buzzards. At Christmas, 1868, Mr Yorke's keepers trapped a common buzzard on Gouthwaite Moor and in 1861 a Mr Ormerod shot a rough-legged buzzard on the moors near Lofthouse.

Up to 1870, Buzzard Scar in Swinnergill (Swaledale) lived up to its name, having a breeding pair of buzzards. Ravens nested nearby and the two pairs of birds engaged in "fierce contests for the possession of the nesting sites." Buzzards were relatively common in Wensleydale in the 1850s. T H Nelson, in The Birds of Yorkshire (1907) wrote: "The gritstone summits and limestone scars of this region [The North-Western Fells] are the last refuge in Yorkshire of the buzzard..."

A Ritualised Slaughter

At halls and mansions throughout the Dales, a collection of stuffed birds was obligatory. Beady-eyed and dusty peregrines, their plumage fading in sunlight, stared out of glass-sided cases. W Eagle Clarke, visiting an eyrie on the north-west fells in 1880, heard that a falcon had been shot on leaving a nest containing four eggs. "She was the sixteenth victim of the gun on this fell," he commented. Seven falcons were reported as destroyed by keepers in Upper Teesdale in 1900 and in June, 1869, game watchers employed by Mr Yorke found, with surprise, the nest of a pair of merlins with four young birds on Ramsgill Moor.

Calluna vulgaris (ling), *Lagapus scoticus* (the red grouse) and *homo sapiens* were the three elements in an extensive man-made landscape. Moorland management included the swizzening [burning] of heather in strips to ensure that each pair of grouse would have heather at various ages, from new growth with succulent shoots to patches of old growth, cover for nests and young. Parliament started its summer break in time for the start of the grouse-shooting season, on August 12, when a titled landowner and his friends shot until the barrels of their guns were hot.

An exponent of this type of moor-rage was Lord Walsingham, who on Blubberhouse, on August 28th, 1872, shot for 12 hours and bagged 842 birds. Twenty beaters were employed, in two parties of 10 each, for 16 drives, the guns used being a pair of breechloaders and a pair of muzzle-loaders.

A fourth element in the moorland pattern was the poacher. Richard Kearton (1926) mentioned that "in the spacious olden times of a hundred years and a little more ago, gangs of miners used to roam the countryside shooting grouse and robbing isolated farm-houses in defiance of law and authority, until they were threatened with a round-up by the red-coats. They [the miners] had a song written in praise of their lawless performances." He had heard it sung when he was a boy, but all he remembered of it was the chorus, which ran:

The miners of Weardale are all valiant men,
And will fight till they die for the bonny moor-hen.

Conditions had calmed down when Major Yorke and his brothers visited Bewerley, in Nidderdale, in the languid days before the 1914-18 war and, being allowed to travel up to Ramsgill Moor with the guns in August, saw true moorland before, here and elsewhere, it was wrecked through overstocking by sheep. Simpson, the head keeper, had amazingly sharp eyes for birds on the wing. He would arrange for his under-keepers to drive grouse along flight lines and would cull the old birds, which, in October, were identifiable by little more than the bold red wattles and the darkness of the plumage.

Tick, heather beetle and the insidious spread of bracken beset the moors today. Farmers used to mow bracken as bedding for the young cattle. In an area of upper Nidderdale, those who wished to mow lined up against a wall and at a signal from the estate agent they rushed forward to stake a claim and to remove the bracken from within a circle of the point first claimed. Demarcation disputes between mowers sometimes led to blows being exchanged.

Black Game

The black grouse was never as common as its cousin, the red grouse and, indeed, had a special mention in estate records. In the game book of Sir Thomas Frankland (1798), with regard to the Blubberhouse estate, it is related: "Pullan, keeper, says that when a boy he shot nine Blackgrouse one morning on these moors, and that his mother made them into a pie for the haymakers." During a period of decline at about that time, John Yorke released some birds in the Pateley Bridge area of Nidderdale but they did not survive.

Richard Kearton commented: "Although upper Swaledale does not present ideal conditions for this species in the shape of birch woods and other forms of cover, a pair suddenly appeared near Muker about fifty years ago and established a footing. The descendants of these birds have thriven and spread in the most remarkable manner." An old-established lek lay between West Stonesdale and Tan Hill.

Gurt Bill (William Alderson, of Angram, upper Swaledale) recalled for me when black grouse in appreciable numbers descended on thorn trees to dine on the berries when food on the hills was sparse. Black grouse were relatively common in the early stages of afforestation at Greenfield, to the north of Penyghent. Among the last areas to have a good population of black grouse was the upper Hodder valley, around Stocks reservoir.

James Usher (1874-1951), for years a gamekeeper at Malham Tarn, befriended naturalist and bird photographer Frank Lowe, who lived at Bolton, and proved to be a man who had a respect for wild life, not just grouse. Incidentally, Usher was married to Mary, a kinswoman of Richard and Cherry Kearton. The grouse moor above Darnbrook to Fountains Fell was managed by "Owd Usher", assisted by William Lund, known locally as Mowdy Bill through his prowess as a mole-catcher.

Usher, who was not a callous man, was delighted when Frank set up a hide close to the nest of a great-crested grebe at the Tarn and invited him to occupy it and see at close quarters a ruby-eyed water bird. Usher, having found the nest of a pair of golden plover, accompanied the naturalist on to the hill and, using a spade, constructed round him and his camera a hide made of peat so that he might photograph the bird.

Change and Decay

Changes in pastoral farming, and in particular a process of mechanisation, then a switch from haymaking to silage, had a profound effect on Dales bird life. The old sward was ripped up during misguided ploughing in the 1939-45 war. Later, with the emphasis on milk production and with the number of cattle climbing steeply, there was re-seeding with ryegrass to provide a quick and early flush of grass to be taken as silage. A second cut might be taken in summer. Land drainage robbed waders like lapwing and redshank of the damp places in the fields to which they led their chicks to dine on insects and worms.

In olden time, hay-making took place in July, by which time the ground-nesting birds had reared their young. When machinery was horse-drawn, a thoughtful farmer attempted to avoid the nests or young of ground-nesting birds. It was known for some farmers, on finding the nest of a pair of daker-hens [corncrakes], to leave an island of grass in an otherwise mown meadow so the birds might rear their young. The heyday of the corncrake in the Dales was from 1800 to 1850, and there were plenty of birds to be heard up to the 1939-45 war. Even when the corncrake was common, this ten and a-half inch long bird, yellowish-buff to brown, with chestnut-coloured wings, was rarely seen. In late April and May, the rasping *crex-crex* of this surreptitious bird was heard mainly at night, the peak of calling being after midnight and until the early hours.

The last corncrake at Austwick, in 1952, was brought out of a meadow in the mouth of a local dog. The bird was released in a local garden; it ran briskly to a herbacious border and was not seen again. The corncrake was heard in a meadow near Sedbergh in 1953 and in the following year three pairs hatched young near Reeth, in Swaledale. One or two pairs nested in the Sedbergh area up to the mid-1960s.

Fifty years ago, when I commuted between Skipton and Clapham, in North Craven, a pair of curlews nested in almost every meadow. Mechanisation had not reached the stage at which half-grown young were being packaged in bales of hay by farmers working so fast they had no time to look out for birds. Travelling by bus I was able to look over the walls. Where fields had been newly cleared of hay, I would see adult curlew and their still earthbound young feeding in the fields.

Fewer in Number

Delius, the Bradford-born composer, who in his young days had a special fondness for Upper Wharfedale, gave us a lyrical *On Hearing the First Cuckoo in Spring*, with its evocation of sunlight on a quiet landscape. The cuckoo is less common than it was. Incidentally, it is the male cuckoo which gives the familiar call (the female utters a series of bubbling notes). When calling, the bird droops its wings, outspreads the tail and holds its head high for the *cuck* and low for the *oo*. Having mated, the male is at liberty to leave the dale-country. The female leaves at about the same time having found small bird hosts for her dozen or so eggs. Astonishingly, long after their parents have left, the young cuckoos find their own way to wintering grounds south of the Sahara and, if they are fortunate will return to the Dales in the following spring.

The spread of the oystercatcher from its traditional seaside habitat to inland areas is an example of natural changes. This black and white bird has an orange-red bill that prompted one observer to think it was holding a carrot! The movement to inland nesting grounds was observed in the early 1920s when oystercatchers from the West Coast entered the Aire Gap, some 30 miles from the sea. In the Dales, breeding was first noted in 1936, when a pair nested by the upper Aire. In 1943, breeding was suspected on shingle on the Swale. Birds were breeding by the Wharfe in 1944 and by the Ure at Aysgarth in 1946.

In Craven, some pairs of oystercatchers chose to lay their eggs in a depression between the six-foot, the space between two railway lines near Gargrave and in the Wenning valley near Bentham. A pair that attempted to breed at Malham Tarn, 1,200ft/360m, in 1978, was not successful. A six mile stretch of the Ribble surveyed in 1972 held 10 pairs, but only two pairs had chosen to nest on riverside shingle; the rest were in nearby fields. Early nests had been washed away by sudden floods.

The state of the rivers has caused concern to anglers who suspect that the seepage of artificial fertilisers from the land into adjacent watercourses, which has produced an abnormal algal bloom and reduced oxygen levels, has led to fish losses and may also be responsible for smaller numbers of ducklings.

Goosanders and cormorants, with prodigious appetites for fish, are now taking trout introduced by angling associations, the cormorant having turned to inland waters following a dearth of coastal fish. The goosander now breeds in the Dales. In one case, a beech tree, rotted at one side, was selected for the nest and anyone peering into this area might see the bird sitting on a soft cushion of leaf litter. Young birds, some 48 hours old, have the impulse to leave the nest. One Dales goosander family left the nesting tree in as little as 24 hours. The cormorant, on its hunting forays, is inclined to roost inland and is seen in quite high numbers on an islet in Stocks reservoir.

With at least 20 pairs nesting in the Yorkshire Dales, the peregrine has recovered from the situation in the early 1960s when, exposed to acute poisoning following the use of highly toxic insecticides, aldrin and dieldrin, which were used as cereal dressings, there were fears for its long-term survival. Pigeons ate the seed and the peregrine ate some of the pigeons. A voluntary ban on spring-sown seed, which had been treated with these two substances, led to a gradual recovery of peregrine numbers. Modern threats are not so much from rock-climbers, who are legally bound not to interfere with nesting areas, but from the egg-collector and, to a limited extent, the falconer.

The collared dove, a conspicuous resident in many Dales towns and villages, is easily identified having a creamy pink-grey plumage, a long tail and a black half-collar at the neck. This greatly extended its breeding range, crossing Europe during the 1930s and arriving in Yorkshire during the late 1950s. By 1975, the species was in the Dales, with doves being seen near Settle and Grassington. Now its dreary cooing is heard in every urban area.

Regular Rarieties

The nightjar, a nesting species with a limited range in the Dales, is heard as well as seen where heather and conifers give a dark grandeur to the uplands around Brimham Rocks, above Nidderdale. Superstitious folk believed they embodied the souls of unbaptised infants and were doomed to fly around forever. Few in number, nightjars take to the air like dark hawks, which have white spots on their wings and tails. The birds wheel and zig-zag with their mouths gaping, trawling for moths and beetles.

The flight call of the nightjar is a sharp *cu-wick* and during its courtship the bird brings its wings together above its back on the upstroke with a clapping sound. Then, alighting on a branch or brush it utters a delicate churring song, the sound rising and falling in pitch, continuing for minutes on end. On moonlit nights they might, like flycatchers, dart out from perches to snatch passing prey. At about six weeks, young nightjars are forced out of the nest to fend for themselves.

Among the "regular rarities" is the osprey, which is seen in passage at reservoirs such as Gouthwaite in Nidderdale and Stocks in the upper Hodder. Four ospreys visited Gouthwaite on the spring passage of 1997. Ospreys in the first wave of returning birds seldom linger. They follow the river valleys northwards to secure the best Scottish territories. Nesting in the Dales surely cannot be long delayed. Dotterel on northward migration are regularly seen on Pendle and Ilkley Moor. A visitor to the Apostle Stones in the middle of Ilkley Moor, in May, 1997, found himself in the company of 19 of these uncommon birds.

An estimated 50% of pairs of hen harriers breeding in England do so on estates owned by North West Water in the Forest of Bowland. In 1997, out of seven nests, three failed, one was washed out by heavy rain and the other two robbed by egg collectors. Another seven pairs of hen harriers were displaying on the Duke of Westminster's estate in the same area but no young were raised in 1997. The Canada goose has for long adorned the lakes of stately houses. During the 1950s and 1960s, Canada geese began to nest on moorland above Gouthwaite reservoir, a scattered colony being found on Dallow Moor, at around 1,000ft/305m. High-level breeding occurs on several moors around the head of Nidderdale, at 1,500ft/450m.

The Changing Dales

Much of the pleasure of bird-watching comes from the unexpected, such as when a glossy ibis, doubtless from some private collection, was seen flying over Kex Gill Moss, near Blubberhouses. The sight of a juvenile rough-legged buzzard in Nidderdale in August prompted speculation that a pair of birds had actually bred in the dale-country. Two pairs of common buzzards, breeding in Upper Nidderdale in 1997, each produced at least two juveniles.

There has been an influx of crossbills into Britain from the Continent. Like waxwings, crossbills have irruptive movement, reacting to food shortages, in this case, a shortage of cones. These large finches, with a *chup-chup* call in flight, have crossed mandibles, an adaptation needed when splitting the outer part of the cone to allow the seed to be extracted. Because crossbills feed their young on conifer seeds, they have a nesting pattern quite unlike other species. They begin the nesting routine in August and raise broods through winter, that being the time when spruce seeds are ripe. In Gisburn Forest, upper Hodder valley, crossbills frequent a large stand of lodgepole pine. A flock of 20 birds was seen feeding on Scot's pine cones at Malham Tarn in June 1997.

In the Dales of today, crows and their relatives have the intelligence to benefit from our affluent society and have an early morning stint rifling litter bins for what remains in fish and chip cartons dumped there during the previous evening. A variant on the pheasant theme is the "Mexican blue", an import from America, the genes of which are now being introduced into the stock by game farms. The only distinguishing mark from the older-style pheasant and this new variety is, to quote a Dales gamekeeper, "a little bit of colour on the back." They are not easy to manage and tend to wander. The ring-neck tends to be a stay-at-home. Poaching pheasants is less common than it was, for the birds are not worth the effort. An estate struggles during winter to get £1 for a brace of pheasants and it costs £2.50 to buy a pheasant at the age of six weeks. The bird has then to be fed.

One bird that keeps away from the haunts of men is the goshawk, fierce hunter of the boreal forest, which has returned to breed in the Dales and has benefited from modern afforestation. Previously, the remnants of the old population had been slain in Victorian times. Snow buntings are still seen in winter and their trilling infuses some life into the dale-country in winter – just as it did in ancient time.

The Mallard, a widespread species

IMAGES OF BIRDS

Stuffed Sheep and Plate Camera

The man who is generally credited with being the "father" of natural history photography was a native of Swaledale. Richard Kearton was born at the compact little village of Thwaite on January 2, 1862, being one of four sons of John and Mary Kearton. His father was a gamekeeper but from yeoman stock, the family having owned land in Swaledale from the 14th century. Under the influence of his forefathers, Richard was soon familiar with the local wildlife. His pride in a Dales background was shared by his publishers who, when Richard's autobiography, *A Naturalist's Pilgrimage*, was published in 1926, described it as "a romance of real life, or how a Shepherd Boy became England's Premier Lecturer." Richard was to describe his native Swaledale as "a pretty valley running like a cartwheel rut between the silent fells of the Pennine Range".

He was physically handicapped from the age of seven when, climbing a tree to reach a bird nest, he fell heavily, dislocating his left hip. The bone-setter at Kirkby Stephen had drunk eight glasses of brandy when he operated on Richard, who lay on a table at a local inn. Two drunken assistants held down the terrified child and no anaesthetic was available to dull his senses. Richard recalled: "He made me much worse. It all ended in my becoming a permanent cripple – and a field naturalist."

Childhood games being beyond his abilities, he spent his time with Old Cherry, his grandfather, who taught him about birds. Grandfather had a sunny disposition and the massive but simple faith of the dalesman. If a servant came in to report the sudden death of the best cow, he would cherrily exclaim: "The Lord giveth and the Lord taketh away; glory be unto His name." Grandfather meant every word of it.

Old Cherry's farm being small, he did some game-watching on the moors. Grandfather never fired a gun in his life "except by accident, and that to the detriment of a rackful of plates in his kitchen." He was a fervent angler who, when he was over 80 years old, with failing eyesight, persuaded young Richard to tie some scarlet wool just above the first "dropper" so he might known when his fishing flies were in the water.

Richard Kearton, who graduated to hobbling with a stick, walked to school at Muker, a mile from Thwaite, his parents paying tuppence a week for his education. He played the usual boyish pranks with his brothers. As the years passed, Richard was able to find the nest of every species of bird breeding in the district. He left school at sixteen and overheard his parents discussing the future of their children - "Jane'll go into service, Jack'll go on to farm; Richard, he's lame – he'll do nowt."

Richard took up farming on Kearton land that fringed Buttertubs Pass, between Wensleydale and Swaledale. The adjacent Muker Moor was rented by one George Brook, who in August, 1882 invited Sidney Galpin to join him for the grouse-shooting. Galpin's father was a founder of the publishing house of Cassell, Petter and Galpin, then the largest publishing house in the world.

The shooting party arrived at Bull Bog, where Richard offered to call up an old cock grouse for Galpin. "We retired to a deep gully in the peat moss and in a few moments I brought along an old moorcock, which was promptly bagged by as pretty a cross shot as I ever saw fired in all my life." Galpin, impressed by the intelligence of the lame boy, offered him a job. That same autumn, Richard took up work in the publicity department at Cassell's.

He had a flair for writing and was invited to write about nests and eggs for Swaysland's *Familiar Wild Birds,* which would be illustrated by the celebrated Archibald Thorburn and others. The work was never completed. Richard was allowed to complete his own part of the work and see it through the press as *Eggs and Egg-collecting,* being paid three guineas for a book that went through 19 editions.

On the death of his father in 1887, Richard persuaded his mother to let his brother, **Cherry Kearton**, join him at Cassell's. Cherry bought a cheap second-hand camera. On April 11, 1892, while the brothers were staying with Yorkshire friends near Enfield, Richard found the nest of a pair of song thrushes and invited Cherry to photograph it. The result was so promising that Richard illustrated his book on bird nests with photographs taken "direct from nature". Those three words were to be the theme of their later work. By chance, the Kearton brothers had founded a new art – that of bird photography. Theirs was the first bird photograph to be reproduced in a book, the honour of taking the first photograph of a wild bird – a lapwing – going to R B Lodge, who used a remote control device in the spring of 1895.

To obtain photographs for a book on *British Bird Nests* they climbed trees, scaled cliffs, ascended mountains and sailed to remote Scottish islands. In 15 years, Richard and Cherry travelled over 30,000 miles and exposed over 10,000 photographic plates. When the book was published in 1895, Richard believed it was the first of its kind to be illustrated entirely by photographs taken "direct from nature". The brothers had taken advantage of the half-tone method of blockmaking introduced from America. Their illustrations showed things as they were – not as they were supposed to be!

The brothers groaned under the weight of photographic material; they worked with a 5in x 4in field camera which had a 9-inch rectilinear lens and a roller-blind shutter. The speed of the plates they used was frustratingly low. They had enormous patience. Cherry spent six days waiting and watching for a series of studies of the kingfisher.

Richard, anxious to obtain pictures of birds without disturbing them, devised "hides" which at first were bizarre – a hollow ox and sheep, part of a tree trunk and an "artificial rock". He subsequently discovered that the actual shape did not matter. Any hollow structure was suitable providing it was introduced at a distance and gradually moved nearer on successive visits.

He also discovered that if two people went to the hide and only one departed, leaving the other inside, the bird to be photographed accepted that danger was over and returned to brood eggs or feed the young.

Tales without number might be told of the resourceful Kearton brothers. They photographed ground-nesting birds from within a stuffed cow, which had the annoying habit of falling over in a stiff wind. They made an artificial boulder, which could be assembled, easily from various pieces. When a shepherd directed them to the nest of a golden plover, Richard covered two hatched chicks with his cap. Then, with "picturesque rashness", he made a sod house five feet away, using the remains of a sheepfold gate as a roof frame and covering it with turves.

A tent, covered with heather, was erected near the nest of a pair of merlins. A stuffed sheep was used as a hide for the camera a few feet from a sandpiper nest and some 50ft of pneumatic tubing was run from it to the stuffed animal. When a shepherd arrived unexpectedly, he sent his dog around the "sheep" and wondered why it did not move –until Richard appeared and explained matters. Cherry Kearton was dangling on a rope beside a cliff where seabirds were nesting when the rope snapped and he fell into the sea. Anxious that the event should have been recorded on film, his first question to those who rescued him was: "Did you photograph me?"

Richard, a popular lecturer who illustrated his words with slides, bought a "moving picture camera" but could not foresee a future for cinephotography. When his lungs began to trouble him, he was advised to get out of London and in about 1898 moved to Caterham. Cherry emigrated to Africa, where he wrote books about wildlife, illustrating them with stunning photographs of big and little game.

Richard died on February 8, 1928, aged 66. Cherry, who eventually returned to England, died in 1940, aged 68. He had just completed a BBC radio broadcast and was on his way home when he had a heart attack. Ralph Chislett, a notable Yorkshire ornithologist, assessed the personality and work of Richard Kearton in these words: "He had the power of entrancing all who met him, but especially – and it was typical of the man – could he bring young people under his spell. By books, pictures and lectures, he did more than any one else to direct the new and growing interest in natural history into the right channels. Among bird photographers he remains the classic master of the art."

Pictures in Miniature

Within my own experience, the work of **Stan Lythe** has been notable not just for the quality of his 35mm pictures but for his love of the Dales. A Leeds man, who was in the fire service for many years, his first effort was at a rookery. This was in woodland on the edge of the city. A bird watcher friend who was an engineer made him a sectional platform from hollow steel. It was bolted to a tree trunk. Using it, recalled Stan, was a hair-raising experience. "I had not realised previously how much a large tree sways in the wind."

From his perch a few yards from nests which are screened from ground level by leaves, he saw tender moments, such as when two birds, perched side by side on a branch, turned towards each other, bowing, their beaks almost touching, their tails fanned and raised over their backs. In early May, when the young were fledged, the platform was dismantled and the canvas hide lowered to the ground. Stan discovered the nest of a pair of blue tits in one of the outside pockets.

I shared some of Stan's adventures in bird photography. The most memorable was when, in autumn, he found the *lek* of black grouse on "white grund" above Malhamdale. In April, with a hide in place, he trained his camera on the prancing blackcock, which displayed with such vigour the grass was pounded into something resembling coconut matting. The main display was a dawn, which was not conducive to good photography nor to a human's sleep pattern. He watched, noted and photographed in the afternoon.

Thin woodland on the hill behind Hubberholme Church, at the head of Wharfedale, held a nesting pair of green woodpeckers. At the time, Stan was helping to improve an old dale cottage and had removed floorboards infested with woodworm. Rather than throw them away, he used them for the hide. The hide did not disturb the routine of the birds as, at hourly intervals, they fed some lusty young.

Stan's main worry was that they might develop a taste for woodworm.

Finding the nest of a pair of short-eared owls by the headwaters of the River Wharfe demanded all Stan's patience and fieldcraft. The adults flew low when hunting and were soon lost to view in the undulations of the ground. In addition, there was little activity around the nest site during the incubation and rearing period. Stan got his pictures – and the owls brought off their young.

Film, Tape and Disc

Colin Preston, FRPS, of Lawkland, is a gamekeeper who, like many another today, is also a conservationist. His knowledge of wildlife and the practical skills that enable him, under licence, to obtain high quality photographs, never cease to amaze me. Needless to say, he obtains a licence for all the projects he plans. He also makes full use of state of the art equipment, an early effort being the attachment of a motor-driven camera to a tripod. He activated a receiver on top of the camera by a transmitter at a range of up to 200 ft. When commanded, the camera would take a photograph – and turn on the film for the next shot! His largest lens is an impressive 800m.

When he found the nest of a pair of curlew in a tussock on moss-land, a hide was erected and moved up to about 15 ft. Colin placed a microphone in the tussock below the nest. He left a small transmitter beside it, the transmission being to a camcorder in the hide. "When the curlew settled down to brood, you could hear the movement of the eggs against each other and, this being the time for hatching, the peeping of the chicks." A photograph taken at this time was one of those which earned him a Fellowship of the Royal Photographic Society. Colin released the shutter of the camera as the curlew on the nest upstretched its neck. In its mandibles was a piece of egg shell. The wings were partly unfurled to reveal a cluster of newly-hatched young. This was most certainly a picture which told a story.

Scaffolding was needed for the photography of buzzards at their large nest on a spruce branch 45 ft above the ground. Colin began to erect a hide – a few yards at a time, over a spell of a fortnight – when the chicks had hatched. Colin spent up to 10 hours at a time in the hide. A friend would "see me in" at 7-30 am and then go to work, returning at 5-30 pm. It was vital that the buzzard should see someone walking away at the start of the vigil. It did not then associate an intruder with the hide.

So constricted was the space that Colin was unable to stand up. He had also to adjust to the swaying motion caused by windy weather. He attached himself to a branch with a rope in case the scaffolding collapsed. Colin spent most of the time with an eye to the camera viewfinder, 13 ft from the buzzard. The bird left for a short spell and gave him the opportunity to open a packet of sandwiches and have a warm drink from his thermos flask. Having a two-way radio, he might also converse with his collaborator.

Colin photographed a pair of tawny owls at night, pre-focussing the camera on the nesting hole in a tree and used a red light in order that he might observe the return of the birds to the nest. Prior to using the red light he had spent a run of three evenings – 17 hours in all – for just one photograph. One bird, which raised special problems, was a pure-white tawny owl. Photographing a white bird in the black of night, he had to work out the exposure with enormous care. Colin took 20 photographs of it – just to make sure there was something worth keeping.

The little owl, with its flattened head and comical expression, is found nesting in some local barns. An appealing photograph taken by Colin shows young birds, their heads protruding from part of the branch of a hollow tree he had sawn down and converted into a nest box. This he had attached to the branch of a rowan tree. It was a picture with no discordant note.

In the use of an infra-red beam to trigger off a camera as a bird passes through, Colin follows a technique which was used effectively by his hero, the late Eric Hosking, and which the pioneers of nature photography would have envied. Infra-red might also be used as a beam interrupter, where a bird in flight activates the trigger and, in effect, photographs itself. Colin is now in the realm of digital recording of bird calls.

MEET THE BIRDS
MOORLAND AND CRAGS

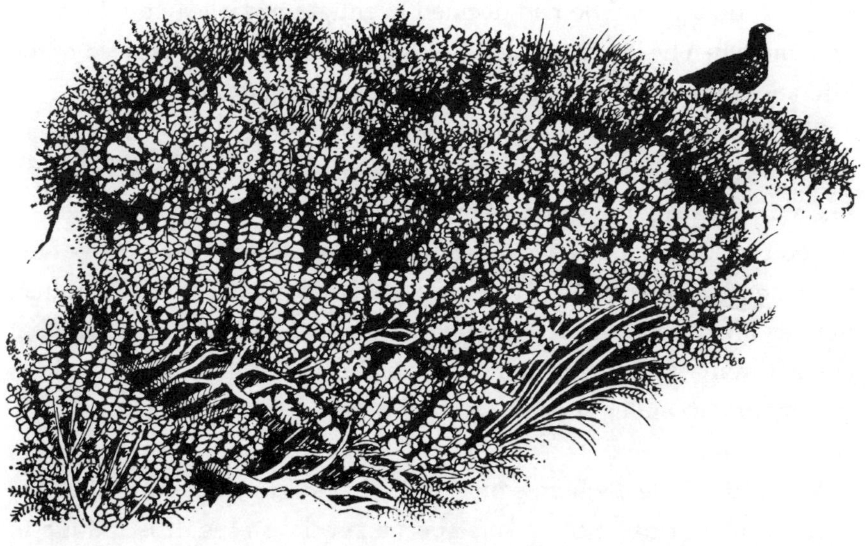

Red Grouse: Monarch of the Moors

Lagopus lagopus

Dales name: Moorcock

Sheep and red grouse occupy the wide hills by the right of over 1,000 generations. With a specialist diet largely composed of heather, the grouse is a prisoner in a shrinking environment – the windswept *Calluna* moors, where ling and clumps of bell heather, associated with bilberry and crowberry, provide a low shrub layer, affording little cover from wind, rain and interlopers. The grouse plucks heather with a short but strong bill. The gut is adapted for dealing with such tough and fibrous plant food.

Disturb a grouse and it will wait almost until the last moment before darting off, fast and low, building up speed with beats of its stubby wings and gliding for short distances. As it pitches down, a testy cock grouse gives a croaky call, *kowa, kowa, kowa*. The sound has the quality of the human voice and has been interpreted as "go back, go back, go back." A dalesman who had decided to emigrate was leaving the family home when he heard a grouse calling "go back". He took heed of the bird and, returning, never left the dale-country again.

The red grouse is well suited to life on the skyline. With a small head, rotund body, rusty-brown plumage and white feathered legs, like avian spats, it merges with the russet tones of the moors. A female in good condition may have a rich honey tone. If a grouse survives the chick stage and grows up to evade the sportsman's shot in August, then its life expectancy is probably two and a-half years. To reach that age is a remarkable achievement considering the bleak environment, the rigours of winter and the starvation period as winter gives way to spring.

We in the Dales, where some of the finest grouse moors are to be found, take pride in the bird's special special status. It is unique to Britain, a local variant of the willow grouse that has a wide distribution across northern lands. The willow grouse dons a white plumage for the winter but our grouse remains dark the year through, though a few white spots hint at the bird's ancestry. The willow grouse is smaller than the red – and is perhaps not so good to eat.

Red grouse and grouse shooting are interwoven in the life of the Dales. On a well-managed moor, the grouse population might reach a high density, with one pair to seven acres. On unkeepered land, as in some parts of the Lake District, there may be one pair of grouse to 200 acres. If left entirely to nature, the moors would quickly revert to woodland. The browsing of sheep prevent the natural regeneration of timber. They also keep the ling well-trimmed and suitable for hungry grouse.

The sporting aspect began when shooters sent trained dogs a little way ahead to "point" at crouching grouse, which were then flushed and shot. Another ploy was to fly a kite to encourage grouse to lie until the last moment, the grouse responding to the kite as they would have to a hawk. Grouse-driving came in with the development of breech-loading guns and was in early use on the Teesdale moors.

Matthew Cherry, a native of upper Swaledale, told me that his grandfather, a moorland gamekeeper, found his territory had been heavily poached by lead miners, a group being known as the the Weardale Gang. Once, in a battle with the off-comers, a gamekeeper had his shoulder broken from a blow struck with a muzzle-loader. Lead-miners poached in their spare time at the week-end or on their days off, even on moonlit nights. When a full moon was due, a Swaledale gamekeeper sat on the opposite side of the valley to his moor, listening for poachers. It was said that because lead-miners worked in semi-darkness they had especially good night eyes.

Poachers were known to drag nets across a moor at night hoping to capture some grouse. Gamekeepers retaliated by setting up thorn trees and snagging the nets. To discourage poaching, miners were offered a day's grouse-beating. . If miners claimed that farmers were getting more jobs than they were, the fretful men would resort to poaching, destroying grouse nests or firing the moor. Some poachers were able to "call" grouse. When birds were pairing, one man keen to bag some birds would imitate the cry of the hen grouse and attract the swaggering moorcocks.

The number and condition of the "moorcock" are directly attributable to the state of the moor. In spring, the moor is swizzened [burnt] to destroy rank heather and to encourage the appearance of fresh shoots. Burning is done in strips, so that at any given time a tract of moor has heather of varying ages, the oldest being capable of providing cover for the birds and their nests. A Swaledale farmer told me: "If it's not dry, it's varra bad to burn."

In winter, the grouse has little company – just the crow, wren and high-stepping fox. Cock grouse are establishing territories as early as November and in January you might see a fight taking place, with feathers flying. The fittest birds have the best ground. A grouse without a good territory will assuredly starve during the winter. Only in the grimmest winters have grouse been known to vacate the moors, appearing at mooredge farms and villages.

Red grouse do not appear to be influenced by the severity of the winter, providing the snow does not have a crust of ice that prevents the birds from reaching the heather. There is normally so much heather available the grouse eat maybe 10 per cent of the standing crop. Years ago, in a protracted snowtime, a Dales gamekeeper arranged for the snow to be "brayed" with a besom to open up food supplies and discourage grouse from migrating down-country, never to return. In summer the sheep go for the high quality grasses but in late winter all those grasses have become exhausted and in snowtime the sheep have to switch to the heather.

The ling is not very nutritious, particularly in early spring, so the hen bird has to eat a good deal, daintily pecking at the growing tips. On some moors, particularly the high wet moors on the Pennine "tops", she often switches to mosscrop [the flowers of cotton grass] because, at that time of the year, the protein content is higher than with heather.

If the winter is relatively kind and frosty weather not prolonged, the new heather growth has a good start, providing a hen grouse with the nutrients she needs to produce good clutches of eggs. The dozen or so eggs she lays represents about 30% of her body weight. Dr Peter Hudson, who studied red grouse intently from a base at Askrigg, in Wensleydale, told me: "It's like an average woman producing a three stone baby." Food reserves are also needed for the task of sitting the eggs for about 27 days.

Spring is tardy on the Pennines. When conditions are spring-like far down the dale, winter maintains its grip on the moor. From the north-east comes snow. From the east come those cold, drying winds which sweep the already impoverished heather and shrivel it, leaving brown patches where it has been destroyed. The few creatures that stir on the moors during the lean days are moving between the cores of old snow-drifts. Foxes dine on grouse when the numbers are high. A fox might sneak up on a grouse and grab it during the day or wait to catch a bird when it is roosting.

In spring, the male grouse advertises its presence by fluttering into the air and descending with fast-beating wings and outspread tail, calling as it descends. By April, the territories of the strongest grouse are secure and the hen birds within them are incubating eggs in nests situated in heather which is usually from 12 to 18 inches high. The cock grouse, on sentry duty up to 70 yards from the nest, warns his mate of any intrusion. A cock grouse spends much of its time being alert to the sounds and sights of the moor. During the nesting season, a sitting bird might not escape attention, though hormonal changes mean that it has no characteristic taste or smell. It relies on immobility and its cryptic coloration.

A ground-nesting bird like a grouse has the attention of stoats and weasels. The carrion crow will take a grouse egg, given a chance A few cock grouse, usually called "rogues", are astonishingly bold. Walkers on the Coast to Coast route through Swaledale have encountered such a bird which, far from flying, has kept them close company. On moorland near the Lancashire border, the territory of a cock bird extended to an unfenced moorland road. The cock grouse appeared to detest red cars and, if one appeared, flew alongside it for several hundred yards.

A cock grouse helps neither with the nest-building nor with the incubation of the eggs. That task is undertaken by the hen, who rarely leaves the nest. Dr Hudson's researches, aided by tiny radio transmitters attached to selected birds, indicate that she is away from the nest for between two and 15 per cent of the time. A clutch consists of nine or 10 eggs, but in a remarkable instance, during the spring of 1979, when many strange things happened on the moors, one nest contained 18 eggs. It was a case of two hen birds laying in the same place. Both birds brooded the eggs, sitting side by side but facing in opposite directions.

Eggs on the lower moors hatch about May 15th and those on the higher moors about the 22nd. The hen grouse eases her chicks out of the shells and the hatched chicks stand round her. So well is the hatching process synchronised that all the chicks emerge within 24 hours. They are promptly led away from the nest site, where the egg shells might attract the attention of predators. Eggs which do not hatch out to time are usually forsaken and the hen bird goes off with the main brood. The crucial period for the chicks is the first 10 days. For the first two days, they live off the yolk sac.

If the weather in late May and June is dry and warm, insect life is abundant and the chicks can move about. In rainy spells, they must be brooded, for they cannot control their own temperature, and little time is spent feeding. In ideal conditions of warmish, dampish weather, the young grouse snap up insects crawling to the tops of the vegetation. Longer journeys are undertaken to boggy areas, with the chicks negotiating humps and hollows on the moor. The hen bird, weak and thin, having "bred herself into the ground", does not relax her vigil for predators.

The precocious chicks put much of their energy reserves into developing their flight feathers. At the age of from 10 to 12 days, a chick might jump into the wind and cover a moderate distance. If a predator appears, the brood scatters, so that no more than one chick is vulnera-

The Red Grouse, also known as the "Moorcock"

ble to attack. Disturb a chick so that it gives an alarm call and you might find that a number of hens and some cocks produce a distraction display, running round with "broken wings", or even running round your feet.

By early June, the days seem endless and the nights are never really dark. The young birds, finding good feeding areas where the ground is boggy, and the concentration of insects highest, quickly gain weight and strength. The cock birds, ever alert, move with the family groups. Not until autumn will they break away from the mixed company and establish territories for the lean days ahead. In July, when there is still a conspicuous difference in size between adults and young, grouse may leave the heather to dine on the seeds of bent and to enjoy the bounty of moorland fruits, such as crowberry and bilberry. In bad weather, they pack.

On what to sportsmen is the Glorious Twelfth (of August), the start of grouse shooting, the human "beaters" drive the grouse towards the butts, where the marksmen are concealed. The coveys are often dense. There is a survival value in a high number. A sportsman with a gun can fire only twice and it has been known for a man to aim at a mass of birds – and claim none of them. Single birds that are shot might be old or diseased.

Go to the moor early on an October day and you see cock grouse displaying and uttering their evocative calls. Dr Hudson believes that many of these "territorial displays" are for the purpose of attracting females. In a spell of bad weather, the grouse form packs. With an improvement in the weather, the cock birds are soon back on their selected grounds. By March and April, available territories have been taken up and most of the birds have paired. If there is a late snowfall, the tracks made by cock birds, which have been displaying and fighting, are clear to see. Red grouse do not have "spurs" but possess some extra "toe-nails" to employ against an adversary.

The red grouse, monarch of the moors, withstands extremes of weather, the pressure of predation and autumnal sport, which does gives the rural economy a monetary infusion and creates jobs. Human interference has raised the population of grouse to far above what it would have been naturally. The shooters and constrictions of the moors do the necessary culling. A disease in grouse that is probably related to the density of birds in previous years is called strongylosis. The cause is a small thread-worm which lives in the bird's gut, being passed out of the bird in its droppings. The worm develops through several stages and then, in wet and warm weather, wriggles to the top of heather stalks and sits there, waiting to be consumed by a grouse, which thus re-infects itself. There is a direct life-cycle, with no intermediate host.

Follow some of the hill roads between Wensleydale and Swaledale and you will see well maintained moorland. In many cases, moors have been debased through overstocking by sheep, especially during and since the 1939-45 war. Afforestation with conifers, so that a few rich people might enjoy tax benefits, has claimed many tracts of moorland. The occasional moorland fire, started unintentionally by a visitor, sterilises the peat and inhibits the growth of heather until erosion removes some of the top surface. In the Dales, little erosion may be necessary before the underlying rock-level is exposed.

The red grouse is a survivor. It clings to its *Calluna* homeland. The poaching lead-miners have gone. So, ironically, has the huge population of grouse. At the approach of spring, the waders return to their upland nesting haunts. Golden plover, dunlin, redshank and curlew are among those benefiting from good moorland management. The distribution of golden plover and red grouse is similar. Lose the red grouse and you will also lose the golden plover.

A Peregrine, high-speed hunter of birds

MOORLAND AND CRAGS

Peregrine

Falco peregrinus

Also known as Great Blue Hawk

In flight, a peregrine, which is the largest of the falcons, looks compact but streamlined, with long and pointed wings and a short tapered tail. The shape is something like a crossbow. An adult bird is a dark blue-grey on the upper parts. The breast and lower parts are creamy-white, barred with black. A juvenile bird has a brown mantle and there are dark brown streaks on the light-coloured underparts. A moustachial stripe, the principal adornment, gives this Dales knight-errant the appearance of Flying Office Kite. The female (falcon) is larger than the male (tiercel).

Derek Ratcliffe, a Cumbrian whose special love has been for hill birds, wrote: "The peregrine has some claim to be regarded as the most exciting and glamorous of all our upland species." On a cliff, the peregrine is safe from terrestrial predators, such as the fox, and it has an unhindered view.

There are now some 20 nesting pairs of peregrines in the Yorkshire Dales and others are seen in Bowland where, with a shortage of sites on crags, a case of ground-nesting has occurred. Arrangements are sometimes made in the Dales for visitors to view nesting activity from a hide set at a distance. Inquire locally about this. Competition for nesting sites is now so intense that peregrines are inclined to stay in the area instead of following tradition and wintering by the coast, where they prey on massed waders. It is from such travels that the word "peregrination" is derived.

The springtime display is exciting to watch. The tiercel circles broadly round his mate, making rapid changes of movement. At times, only the tips of the wings appear to move. Then a powerful thrust of the angular wings is apparent. Through the air comes a stuttering call – *kee, kee, kee, kee.* If any creature threatens the peregrine's nesting space, it is verbally abused. A bird circles with slow wing beats and utters a ringing series of calls which is audible in the next parish. The nest, on a ledge, is sparse indeed. The downy white young eventually assume a juvenile brown plumage.

A peregrine takes fresh meat, caught on the wing. The stoop [dive] of a peregrine on prey is a thrilling sight. The cigar-shaped body reduces drag and the bird might attain a speed of over 100 miles an hour. This bird has been associated with no less than 120 species of bird prey. From evidence of kills found among the litter at nesting sites on the Pennines, the chief prey is the pigeon. On a moor, the peregrine cannot match the grouse's acceleration in level flight (the grouse moves fast and low). Grouse become educated in the ways of local peregrines.

Raven

Corvus Corax

Dales name: Corbie

The raven, largest member of the crow family, has an overall black plumage, though the glossy plumage is shot over with a purplish-green. The male bird is marginally brighter than the female, though this will not be noticeable in the field. In flight, the wedge-shaped tail is a distinguishing feature. At relatively close quarters, notice the ponderous black beak and shaggy throat.

The voice of the raven is a deep throaty croak – *pruk, pruk, pruk.* It is a veritable bass-baritone among bird vocalists. This bird is a superb flier. Nesting on cliffs, where there is usually an uprush of air, it more often glides than flaps its backswept wings. The primaries of the wings are splayed out, like black fingers. The raven has a fine turn of speed when needed. At other times, the bird seems to dawdle in the air, a plaything of the wind.

Ravens pair for life. During courtship, a male soars on a thermal, then suddenly descends with wings well tucked in. The courtship displays find the birds tumbling, climbing and diving. A raven might also momentarily turn on its back in flight. When a raven territory is violated, the agitated birds sweep along the clifftop. One of them, alighting, peevishly tugs up pieces of grass and tosses them to the breeze. An amused observer saw an agitated raven settle on a sheep's back and rip off some wool. On a misty day, a raven will play hide-and-seek with you.

When a sheep dies because it cannot face up to the winter blast or is afflicted by one of the many diseases to which humans have given strange names like pulpy kidney, ravens feast on the corpses like vultures. The nest of the raven is usually made on a cornice, fairly high up on a crag, the elevation ranging from 20ft to 50ft. Some nests that are used annually become very large, but usually a pair in its territory rings the changes of several sites. The bulky nest is constructed of twigs from hawthorn, rowan and heather or any such material that is handy. Sheep wool is used to line the cup.

Nesting takes place so early in the year that in a few cases eggs have been found in February. By the third week in March, incubation is in progress. Often, a sitting bird on its high crag is pelted by hail or powdered white by snow. The incubation period is about 21 days and the fledging period takes from five to six weeks, occurring during lambing time at the hill farms and ensuring a good supply of carrion food from deceased sheep. A single nestling, having the undivided attention of its parents, flew just three weeks after hatching. Single birds are usual where the breeding stock is young or very old. A young raven calls with a crow-like *karr*.

The birds need plenty of space in which to feed, their sharp eyes locating the corpses of sheep and lambs. When not out and about with their young in summer, ravens stay in their territories. Young birds or non-breeding pairs roost communally. Such a floating population is thought to contain a surplus of potential breeders, for usually if one of a nesting pair dies, another quickly takes its place. Some young ravens from the northern Pennines winter in the Dales.

Wren

Troglodytes troglodytes

Dales name: Chitty

The wren is included among the cliff-nesting birds because this tiny bird might be seen in a rocky gorge where there is some vegetation as well as beside a lowland lonnin (lane). Anyone who has possessed a farthing will be familiar with the appearance of the wren. It is a tubby little bird, with a russet-brown plumage, which is barred, particularly over the wings and flanks. The wren has a relatively big head, longish beak and cocked-up tail, which shows an affinity with the dipper, to which it is most closely related.

This diminutive species might be found nesting in crevices in cliffs, in stone walls, hedgerows and hollow trees. A wren, a mere 3 ½ inches in length, feeds mainly on the larvae of moths, flies and beetles. In springtime, a wren in its territory has a favourite song perch and fills the air with loud, vehement notes. The run of notes is also given as a mating song. A churring sound is the wren's alarm call.

The male makes several nests and then invites the female to select one. A nest is spherical and formed of roots, moss, grass and leaves, being lined with feathers.

Jackdaw

Corvus monedula

Dales Name: Jack

The smallest member of the crow family is not over-awed by the others. A jolly bird, it moves jauntily through life, forever shouting its name – jack-jack – shrill and clear. From a distance the jackdaw appears to be black. At closer quarters you will notice that the sides of the head, the nape and underparts are grey.

In winter, large flocks of noisy jackdaws moving from roost to feeding grounds are most conspicuous. They may be in the company of rook and starling. Colonial nesting occurs on cliffs. Single pairs exploit unused chimneys and holes in trees. Small colonies are found in unprotected church towers.

Merlin

Falco columbarius

Dales name: Stone-Falcon

The merlin, our smallest bird of prey, is about the size of a mistle thrush. This is a true falcon, with a streamlined appearance, pointed wings and shortish tail. The male has a blueish plumage and the female is brownish. That's as much as you are likely to see in the wild, for the merlin moves fast and low and is inconspicuous during the nesting season. Its call is an urgent quic-ik-ik-ik.

The Dales and Bowland are a stronghold of the merlin population. Nesting takes place in moderately tall heather on slightly sloping ground, usually where there are scattered rocks, one of which will form a popular perch. The species has been studied intently on the Barden Moors of the Bolton Abbey estate in Wharfedale.

The chief prey item being the meadow pipit, it is surprising that any pipits remain on the moor. The merlin singles out a small bird in flight and pursues it, following every twist and turn until, if successful, it rises above its prey and makes the final stoop. On a favoured moor, there might be four or five pairs of merlins, each rearing about four chicks and each pair bringing to the nest at least 10 meadow pipits a day for a month, in addition to the food needed by the adult birds.

The average clutch of four is incubated for about a month, incubation beginning with the laying of the first egg, which means the chicks are of various sizes. On first hatching, the young are covered with grey down, except for the crown of the head, which is almost white. In another month, the chicks are fledged.

In winter, the moors are vacated by merlins, the birds switching their attention to the massed wading birds at the coast.

Golden Plover

Pluvialis squatarola

Dales name: Whistler

A golden plover, described as "the spirit of the moors", returns in spring with a dark back flecked with gold. A light band separates the mantle from the brown underparts. In the northern race birds, which might be seen in the dale-country before they return to Iceland to breed, the underparts are coal-black. The flight call of a golden plover, tlui, is musical but somewhat mournful. Ian Appleyard likened the alarm call to "the opening of a rusty gate".

The Yorkshire Dales hold seven per cent of the national golden plover population. It is not unusal to find the species nesting at an elevation of over 1,500ft/450m. Flocks appear in upland pastures in February and March and some courtship activity might be noticed before they disperse to their high-lying nesting areas. A cold spell persuades them to fall back on lower ground.

The bird has dash and verve, but the spring display flight of a male above its nesting territory is performed in slow motion. The wings move stiffly, in, out, with half a second for each stroke. The bird will then fly rapidly for a short distance.

Golden Plover

The bird is devious when danger threatens and by the time it appears to your view it will already be well clear of the nest. Notice the small head, upstretched neck and plump body, which collectively give the impression of a long-necked wine bottle. The bird calls several times, moving with swift steps to another vantage-point, where it will call again. Sometimes only the head and neck are visible over a ridge. When reaching down for food, a golden plover tilts its whole body.

Golden plover chicks are covered with down that looks as though it has been sprinkled with pepper. Ralph Chislett (1946) wrote: "Newly-hatched young are clothed in down speckled with the same gold that spangles the shawl the old birds wear across their shoulders."

Dunlin

Calidris alpina

Dales name: Purre

This small, jolly little wader has a nuptial plumage featuring a chestnut mantle and light underparts. In the nesting season, both sexes have a black patch beneath. The bill is slightly curved. In winter, when the dunlin has a greyish plumage, our muddy coastlines teem with dunlin from northern lands.

The dunlin, which is like a smaller version of the golden plover and has a similar type of nesting haunt, is sometimes referred to as "the plover's page". Thinly spread on the Pennines, the dunlin is found mainly where there is standing water, such as peaty pools or a small tarn, where it derives its food. A dunlin is the most confiding of the waders, this manner being effective when distracting the attention of enemies from its nest.

Our summer visitors return to nest in April. The amorous male, in the presence of the female, assumes an upright posture, and puffs up the breast feathers, displaying to the best effect the black patch that is a prominent feature of its nuptial plumage. When displaying in flight, the male alternates between gliding and beating its wings fast, the wings being down-curved at the time. The bird utters a purring trill which is so haunting, yet so light, it makes a curlew call seem an intrusion and the becking of red grouse downright coarse.

The dunlin nests much later than the golden plover, the season occurring from late May or early June. The nest is set in a tussock and is lined with stems or leaves. The male takes an increasing share of incubation and the female is inclined to leave the area before the eggs hatch in about three weeks. The male invariably deserts the brood before they have fledged.

Black Grouse

Tetrao tetrix

Dales name: Heath Cock

Black Grouse

Black grouse prefer marginal areas such as woodland fringes and marshy uplands. The male bird, known as the blackcock, is a large, handsome, blue-black bird, with red eye wattles. Males gather in the early morning and also at times in the evening to display at open "leks", where they posture, call and leap up and down in an effort to attract a visiting female, known as the grey-hen, though in fact she is brown, with black barrings. Black grouse, once locally common in the Dales, are now quite rare.

The portly blackcock, weighing about 4 lb., greets each new day, mainly in April, with a protracted display in which birds face each other in pairs at an assembly place known as a *lek,* from the Swedish leka, meaning "to play". A diurnal clock brings black grouse together from widely different places at about the same time. Explosive sounds are uttered. After a challenging *tchie-whai,* birds face each other in pairs and prance about. A series of gentle bubbling pigeon-like notes known as *roo-cooing* is heard. Thus does a black grouse caution the other bird which might step over an invisible line marking one territory from another. Hissing, wheezing, sneezing, cooing – the vocabularly is varied and strange to those humans who are out of bed early enough to hear it. Physical movements designed to make a bird look impressive support the fervent calling.

The crimson wattles above the eyes are inflated and neck feathers raised until they are almost like a ruff. Head and bill point upwards. The lyre-shaped tail is fanned out, revealing a rosette of white feathers which normally rests below it. The wings and outer tail feathers droop. For *roo-cooing*, a bird lowers its head and neck until they are almost horizontal and a few inches above the ground. The throat is distended with air, like a bagpipe, the air being gulped in by a rapid opening and closing of the bill.

Scuffles occur between rival cocks. They "see-saw", one bird extending head and neck towards its rival, which draws back. As the first bird retracts its head, so the partner's head is extended. These forward-and-backward movements are synchronised and enacted several times in rapid succession.

Any females arriving to be mated are attracted to the mature, more vigorous birds in the central positions. The appearance of a greyhen leads to a battle between males, which might even throw themselves over a foot in the air and strike out with their claws like gamecocks. When the greyhens have been mated, they are on their own, making their nests in a tangle of vegetation, incubating eggs and rearing the chicks without masculine help. When leaving a nest, which is not often, the greyhen covers her eggs with bits of the surrounding vegetation, so the nest, partly hidden in any case by overhanging plants, is always difficult to find.

Dales gamekeepers have told me of leks attended by over 30 cocks. Matthew Philipson, a bird-watcher on the northern Pennines early this century, saw as many as 40 blackcocks arrayed at the lek. He added: "I myself have often seen packs of 50 on the hawthorn hedges during the winter months and, on a single morning, have counted 150 birds, all within a square mile of ground." Black grouse regularly appeared on the dinner tables of the hill farmers. A Swaledale farmer told me that a black grouse "has three different colours o' flesh – pink, then white, then rather dark. It's a solid bird and good to eat. I was nivver particular how it was cooked; it always seemed to taste good!"

The decline of this species reflects the present sad state of the uplands, where agricultural land has been transformed by planting and re-seeding and woodland regeneration gravely affected by the browsing of many sheep. Fewer than 500 blackcocks are left in England, most of them being found in the north-country uplands. Numbers have been falling at the rate of 10 per cent per year. Only 15 hen birds were counted in the Dales in 1997, when the success of the breeding season was affected by heavy rain in mid-June.

Meadow Pipit

Anthus pratensis

Dales name: Ling Tit

An unspectacular little song bird, the meadow pipit is olive brown, with a thin bill and white sides to the tail. It has a streaky breast and resembles a diminutive thrush.

The pipit pair's territory is large, the innermost part catering for the needs of the adults and a wider area being the feeding ground of the young. The food taken is mainly in the form of insects. A neatly woven nest is set deep in rank vegetation and would be difficult to find if the sitting bird, invariably the female, did not leave it until the last moment to take flight. On being disturbed, the meadow pipit flies high, nervously, calling *tseep tseep tseep.*

In its display, the meadow pipit descends, singing, with wings and tails stiffly extended. It is called the shuttlecock flight. At lower elevations, the meadow pipit is a favourite host of the cuckoo.

Twite

Carduelis flavirostris

Dales Name: Mountain Linnet.

The twite is, indeed, a hill version of the linnet, which it vaguely resembles. In breeding plumage, the male is darkish brown, the underparts being prominently streaked. The rump is pink and the horny bill yellow.

A bird of the heather moors, the twite has declined considerably but the north-country, especially the Central Pennines, is still its stronghold. A breeding pair usually obtains the seeds it needs as food from adjacent farm land. The nesting season is variable, with some birds incubating their eggs in May and others holding back until June. The twite winters at the coast.

Black-headed Gull

Larus ridibundus

Dales name: Nothing recorded.

This common, noisy gull has a red beak. The head looks black but is really chocolate-brown. The dark hood is assumed during the nesting season. The dark feathers of the hood are moulted in autumn, when there is just a dark spot behind each eye. Notice a triangular white "flash" on the forewing.

The raucous cries of the black-headed gulls are continuous at its nesting places, which include an island on Stocks Reservoir. This species is seen in large numbers whenever a field is being ploughed out for re-seeding.

MARGINAL LAND

The Yorkshire Dales have been described as "the landscapes of our upland fringe". An important type of landscape for nesting has been defined as "wet grassland", this being high, rush-infested pastures where curlew, lapwing, redshank and snipe rear their families. Much of this ground was taken in hand during the Enclosures and is termed "allotment". Hard-won by generations of Dales farmers, it is now "going back", as evidenced by gapped walls. The dereliction brought about on the hills by changes in farming practice and by rural depopulation tends to be good for birds.

Curlew

Numentius arquata

Dales name: Whaup (borrowed from the Scots)

Notice the streaky-brown plumage, long neck, relatively small head and a long curved bill, which is well adapted for probing, the bird being able to open just the tip to gather food. The bill of the female is appreciably longer than that of the male. When the bird takes flight, a triangular patch of white at the rump is conspicuous. Alas, the curlew is much less common as a nester than it was 20 years ago. Wintering birds are found on the mudflats of coastal - estuaries.

At Malham, on a truly wet day, a farmer remarked: "It'll rain if you hear an old curlew twarting [calling] at night." The curlew, our largest wader, must do a lot of twarting on Malham Moor, where the average precipitation is 58 inches and the number of days in the year with measurable rain averages 220. The main call, a ringing *cour-lee,* helps to wake up the dale-country in spring. Even more thrilling is the bubbling song, which was said by Lord Grey to be "the most healing sound in nature."

The Yorkshire Dales support 10 per cent of the national curlew population. This bird was the gamekeeper's watchdog. No creature might stir on the moor in spring and early summer without invoking the wrath of the long-nebbed bird. Curlews may be assembling on lower ground as early as February, but they do not usually arrive back in their nesting areas until well into March, the male birds returning first to establish territories within which they court the incoming females. In April, the hills used to ring with curlew calls. It was the curlew, not the cuckoo, which heralded the Dales spring.

When curlews were relatively common, one pair nested on the grass verge of the high-lying road between Settle and Malhamdale. Another pair, nesting inside a young conifer wood, deserted their first clutch of eggs when the female, rising at the approach of an intruder, caught a leg in bramble and was brought back heavily on to the eggs, two of which were broken. The pair nested again – just outside the wood.

Displays at the nesting areas are not elaborate but the curlew enchants us by its bubbling song, which was well described over half a century ago by Ralph Chislett. He noted that the curlew might be heard almost anywhere in the dale country and observed: "As the curlew floats along a hillside, a low whistle comes, slowly repeated between pauses. Then the whistle rises in the scale, becoming shrill and emphatic, with considerable tremolo effect, between each shorter pause. The far-flung top note is repeated a few times; then slowly the scale falls. If the bird has been watched, short rapid upward flights will have been seen to alternate with slow glides as the sound was produced."

The nest is a shallow depression in the ground, sometimes in a tussock, containing a clutch of four large pear-shaped eggs. Some curlews have eggs before the end of April, but most start to lay in about the

The Curlew, a long-nebbed summer visitor to the moors

first week of May, the male helping with the incubation. The curlew is fierce in defence of its chicks and descends on any intruding crows with yelping calls. It none the less suffers from predation. Crows filched eggs from one nest, the remaining egg being sucked by a vagrant hedgehog.

A curlew walks a good distance on to the nest to frustrate any watchful predators and, when alarmed while sitting, a curlew presses against the ground, with neck outstretched and beak held out, remaining motionless until it feels safe again. For about six weeks after hatching, a young curlew is incapable of flight. Many perished under tractor-hauled haytime machines. Another reason for the numerical decline of the curlew is the transformation of many Dales meadows to provide improved strains of grass for silage-making and the taking of two crops of silage. Grubs, larvae and small worms are scarce in areas that teemed with them.

Post-breeding flocks of curlews gather on moorland between Reeth and Leyburn and at Tarn Moss, by Malham Tarn, which sustains quite large flocks of curlews both before and after the nesting season. Over 500 curlews have been counted on the Moss in summer. Well over 1,000 used to be seen on the big fields of the Ribble Valley between Settle and Long Preston. Moulting, a protracted process, may not be completed until December, but as the feathers are cast and re-grown in pairs, the birds' powers of flight are not seriously affected. Dales curlews tend to move south-westwards for winter, some to the estuaries or marshland of Eire. More than one Dales bird has been recovered from land beside the Shannon.

Lapwing

Vanellus vanellus

Dales name: Tewit

The Lapwing

The lapwing is glossy green above and white on the underparts. Notice the long headcrest. At close quarters, and especially as the bird tilts to feed, the chestnut of the under-tail coverts is in clear view. The lapwing's call is a mournful pee-wi. The bird's name is associated with its flight. A flock of birds in characteristically slow flight produces a twinkling effect from the alternation of dark and light surfaces. Lapwings nest in moist areas (known to dalesfolk of old as "tewit grund"). They need good soil cover because of their partiality for earthworms. Lapwings were once revered for consuming insect pests. The birds winter on low land and by the coast.

With its two-tone colour scheme, its plaintive call and rakish head crest, the lapwing is the odd bird out among the waders visiting the Dales to nest. The general scheme is streaky brown. In dull light, the dark green of the lapwing looks black. In bright conditions, it is seen to be shot with bronze and purple.

Lapwings return to the upper dales as early as February. Early in the breeding season the cock birds entertain us by their noisy tumbling flights which at times border on what appears to be recklessness. They tend to be colonial in their nesting areas. A mated pair makes "scrapes" within its territory, one of which will be inconspicuously lined as a nest. When scrape-making, the cock lapwing up-ends. Dipping its breast in a dancing rhythm, the bird holds its wings erect while working its feet hard to press out the saucer-shaped depression.

A clutch of four pear-shaped eggs is laid as early as March, if the weather is mild, but generally it is mid-April before laying begins. Even so, the lapwing sometimes has to sit hard during a springtime blizzard. Lapwings are fearless in defence of their nest, harrying much bigger birds like carrion crows. Collecting lapwing eggs for the kitchen was once a common pursuit in the Dales. The taking of early eggs stimulated a lapwing to lay another clutch.

The chicks are soon mobile, responding in a remarkable way to the warning cries of the parents. Several times I have found chicks crouching in the hoof prints of cows. Because lapwings nest early, flocking occurs when many other waders are still attending to their young. June flocks are presumably composed of failed breeders. When flocking in late summer, lapwings are frequently in the company of starlings.

Short-eared Owl

Asio flammeus

Dales names: Moor or moss owl.

This owl is very un-owl-like, being active by day and nesting among heather on the ground. It is a conspicuous bird and when not in flight might sit on a post like a feathered totem. Notice the long wings, which are swept back. As it silently patrols its territory, on rolling moorland, it resembles a big brown moth. Notice how it wheels and side-slips. In good light, an area of golden-buff is seen on the primary feathers.

The bird is named after ear tufts which are unrelated to the sense of hearing. They are raised only at times of alarm or excitement. In spring, a barking call is heard as a displaying bird "claps" its wings beneath its body. During this noisy tattoo, the bird drops 10 feet or more but quickly regains its trim and flying grace as the wings are outstretched again. The flight is otherwise silent. Even at close quarters, you will have only the evidence of your eyes to tell you where the owl is moving.

Crows harry this gentle-looking bird but the owl invariably leads them in such tight circles the observer may have reason to wonder which bird is being pursued – owl or crow. Nesting is on the ground. The female begins to incubate from the moment the first egg has been laid and rarely leaves the nest until the chicks begin to wander from it. Food is provided by her mate, a smaller, darker bird.

Dawn is a time of hectic feeding. The main prey is the short-tailed field vole, which is cyclical, having periodic years of abundance, especially in areas newly-planted with trees. In a "vole year", a pair of owls might rear a large family. A hunting bird usually decapitates a vole and when there are voles in abundance prey items are laid neatly side-by-side against future requirements.

The precocious chicks move away from the nest not long after hatching and are fed by the adults at dispersal points. Many short-eared owls go to the coast in winter though an occasional winter sighting in the dale-country is possible.

Ring Ouzel

Turdus torquatus

Dales name: Crag Ouzel

Known to many as "mountain blackbird", the ring ouzel is in effect an upland version of the well-known garden bird, but occurs above the 1,000ft/305m contour line and is a summer visitor to the Dales. The blackbird is widespread; the ring ouzel has a local distribution. A ring ouzel's plumage lacks the velvety darkness of the blackbird and the ouzel has a less tuneful song. Dark feathers and a white crescent on the chest signify a male. The female is brownish and the crescent less well defined.

Some ring ouzels return to their Dales haunts in March, having wintered on the Atlas Mountains of North Africa. The main immigration is in early April. Bill Robson, a long time student of Pennine ring ouzels, told me: "The main appeal to me is their preference for the quiet, undisturbed areas of the fells and their fluty, piping calls which, especially in the evening, can create a thrilling atmosphere." Like the blackbird, this ouzel has a nervy manner and a chattering call. Long, pointed wings are used to great effect when flying low in a cluttered landscape.

Steep-sided gills are favourite nesting places and in such a situation the fluty calls of the cock bird resound as in an echo-chamber. It is particularly effective on a calm springtime morning when the bird is singing in the gill, as for example that on the Swaledale side of the Buttertubs Pass. The calls advertise an ouzel's presence, but subsequently the bird might be difficult to locate. When conscious of being watched, it soon takes cover among rocks or in rank vegetation.

The nest, which normally is situated on a ledge low down in a gill, is formed of pieces of dead bracken and rough grasses, lined with finer grasses. Incubation takes 14 days and some handbooks give a similar period as the time for fledging but Bill Robson noted that young ouzels develop more quickly than that, some of them flying at 12 days. When the nest is threatened, the ring ouzel utters a coarse chacking sound.

The breeding haunts of blackbirds and ring ouzels occasionally overlap. At a derelict Pennine farmhouse, a pair of blackbirds built a nest on the kitchen mantelpiece and ring ouzels nested in a shattered bedroom ceiling. It was difficult to distinguish between the two nests and the two clutches of eggs and both were successful. Nests in a gill near Grassington were built on rock ledges near mining spoil heaps. On Mickle Fell, which prior to local government reorganisation in 1974 was the most northerly point of Yorkshire, a pair of ring ouzels built within the shattered fuselage of a crashed aircraft. A new nest was constructed each year, joining a row of nests side by side on an aluminium girder.

Many pairs of ring ouzels are double brooded. At the end of the season, quite small groups of birds range along the fell slopes, feeding on bilberries and later taking the fruit of rowans that grow at lower elevations. Where moorland fruits are plentiful, the birds' droppings are stained purple. The ring ouzels depart from the Dales from late August and through September. It is possible that one or two birds overwinter with us.

Carrion Crow

Corvus corone

Dales name: Ket Crow.

Glossy black, with a black bill, the carrion crow is a handsome, intelligent bird. Generally, the crow is sleeker than a rook and is less sociable, though it will join in communal roosts in winter. The crow's call is a loud "kraar".

The carrion crow is disliked by Dales farmers because of its attacks on rigged (upside down) sheep and weakly or ailing lambs. Gamekeepers know it as a major predator on the eggs and young of ground-nesting birds. A crow has a systematic approach to egg-stealing. One moved from post to post, in an area where a field was edged by rough grass, until it located a partridge nest. This bird also raided pheasant nests, taking the eggs to a place in the wood where the ground was strewn with the shells of sucked eggs.

Now that the shooting pressure on crows has lessened, the species is not as timid of man as was the case when long pokers were used to dislodge crow eggs and any bird which came within gunshot was slain. I regularly see family parties of crows which remain perched on wall or tree as I pass at close range.

A pair of crows nests in a solitary state, often choosing a thorn tree in a gill or at the edge of the moor. A nest, large, of coarse twigs and with sheepbones worked into the structure, is at from 10 to 12 feet from the ground. The eggs repose in a deep, windproof cup lined with hair and sheep wool. In the Settle district, and in the absence of sufficient solitary trees for nesting purposes, a pair of crows built a nest on a wall-top. Even more unusual was the crow in the same area that laid eggs in a wool-lined depression on the ground.

Although eggs have been found before the end of March, it is more likely to be mid-April before the clutch is completed. The nestlings are at first a fleshy-pink, like plucked fowls – all gape and stomach and vent. After a good meal, they loll in the nest until a parent arrives with yet more food. Then each nestling raises its reptillian head and opens its beak, exposing a red gape. As time goes by, the scraggy bodies darken. The nesting tree is by now leafed over, obscuring the nest from viewers on the ground and giving it some cover.

Wheatear

Oenanthe oenanthe

Dales name: Stone Chopper

Look in stony country for the wheatear, which is about the size of a robin and perches on a boulder or capstone of a drystone wall with a smart upright stance. Its call is a hard "chack", as though two pebbles were being tapped together. The male bird, a dandy of the fellsides, has a blue-grey back and crown, a black mask, ochre breast and black wings. A female is a brownish-grey. The species is named after the white patch on the rump. Notice that black feathers on the tail form a letter T.

The wheatear, first of the summer bird visitors to the Dales, winters south of the Sahara yet contrives to arrive back in its nesting haunts in late March, when winter and spring overlap with cold, wet weather. It is a fidgety bird, forever spreading or wagging its tail. The cock bird will flit ahead of you on a drystone wall, playing hide and seek. The bird moves on the ground in a series of long hops, making a sudden fluttering sortie into the air to capture a winged insect.

The nest is in a hole, either a gap among rocks or a deserted rabbit burrow. Numerically, the wheatear is declining, partly because of an increase in birds of prey, a marauding sparrow hawk, now relatively common, finding the boldly marked cock wheatear standing on a wall an irresistible sight.

Redshank

Tringa totanus

Dales name: Red Legs.

One of the streaky brown waders, readily identifiable, especially if perched on a stone wall or fencing post, because of its orange-red shanks (legs). This bird has a prominent red bill.

The redshank's neurotic and noisy manner is revealed if you unwittingly go near its nest, which is on the ground. A fretful redshank bobs its head, then rises steeply, with sharp and shallow wing-beats revealing a patch of white feathers on the rump and white at the trailing edges of the wing.

This species is common at the coast but was little-known in the Dales until this century, when birds began to follow up the rivers and nest in moist meadows. Now there are few of the old-style meadows, the redshank is uncommon.

The bird has a variety of calls, the commonest being a melancholy piping, repeated loudly and at high speed if its nesting territory has been violated. So fervent is its voice, it might be proclaiming the end of the world.

Skylark

Alauda arvensis

Dales name: Laverock

The skylark, a streaky brown bird with a headcrest, is easily overlooked when on the ground or when in low flight. A skylark walks; it does not hop. It has a chirrupy call. A lark in song flight is readily seen as it rises like a feathered helicopter. Though it may be little more than a black spot against the blue vault of the sky, its warbling song is astonishingly loud. The song flight appears to be important in pair-formation.

The skylark is a characteristic species of hill grassland but may also be found at quite high elevation. Though little bigger than a sparrow, it has broad wings and especially light bones and thus can fly and sing rapturously for quite long periods and maintains its position when there is a breeze. The female makes the nest, of grass and leaves, and alone incubates the eggs. The male does even play a part in feeding the young.

The skylark is locally common but with changes in farming practice no longer finds enough cover or food to enable it to nest on the best farmland.

Yellow Wagtail

Motacilla flava

Dales name: Cow Bird

The yellow wagtail is one of three species of wagtail to be found in the damp habitat along the sides of rivers in the Dales. I associate this species in particular with the River Dee, the watercourse of Dentdale, where their numbers are relatively high. The male is a vivid yellow below, with a greenish-yellow crown and mantle. The outer tail feathers are white. The female is duller, paler green and buff-yellow.

A wagging tail is significant, though this bird has the shortest tail of the wagtail family. Its call is a loud and prolonged "tsweep". A yellow wagtail, despite its frail appearance, winters in West Africa. The birds are en route to their nesting areas in mid-April and remain in the Dales until September.

The name "cow bird", from Sedbergh, is derived from its proneness to feed in close company with cattle. Ralph Chislett found a pair of yellow wagtails breeding at 1,700ft/520m in North Ribblesdale. Other pairs were scattered at intervals down to the river.

Snipe

Gallinago gallinago

Dales name: Heather-bleater

A small brown wader with a very long bill (nearly as long as its body). It tends to sit tight and when flushed to rise with a sharp "scaap", which sounds like a sneeze. The bird takes a zig-zag course and the long bill tends to be angled downwards in flight.

This secretive bird of high mossland rests by day and feeds in the evening and at night. From April to June, the male snipe "bleats" as it flies in the weeping grey sky. The tremulous music, which is created mechanically, not vocally, fits the bird's wild environment.

Notice that the snipe alternates between steep climbs and descents. As it dives, air rushing through stiff barbs of the outer tail feathers, which have been extended, create the bleating sound. This is also known as "drumming". Some country children took the two stiffened feathers from a dead bird and whirled them around on a length of string.

Snipe are among the early nesters, the eggs being laid in early to mid-April, the nest being a hollow in a tussock of grass or clump of rushes. Snipe chicks, which are pattered with dark brown and black, are among the most attractive of young waders.

A Dales gamekeeper used to drench some of the mossland with blood obtained from abbatoirs. This created a particularly succulent type of worm, atttracting a large number of snipe in winter. A snipe, probing muddy ground with a bill, which has a sensitive tip, registering contact with small, solid items, does not actually see the food it swallows.

RIVERS, TARNS AND RESERVOIRS

The main rivers of the Yorkshire Dales – Swale, Ure, Wharfe, Aire and Nidd – extend like fingers from a palm represented by the Plain of York. Of the reservoirs, the largest expanse of water is Grimwith, between Hebden and Greenhow Hill. More interesting to bird-watchers, especially in winter, are Gouthwaite (Nidderdale) and Stocks (upper valley of the Hodder). Two large tarns of note are Malham Tarn and Semerwater.

Grey Heron

Ardea cinerea

Dales name: Heronsewe

Though mostly grey, this large waterside bird is white on the neck and breast. Black stripes about the eyes develop into a pennant-like crest. The throat and breast are marked by dark streaks. Nesting is usually colonial, in the tops of tall trees, a group being known as a heronry, but some pairs in the Dales nest alone or with one or two other pairs.

Three feet long, mostly legs and neck, the heron is not a bird to be ignored, though as it stands at the riverside, waiting for fish to come in range of its spear-like beak, it resembles a grey post. In flight, the neck is drawn back, the wings are arched and the legs extend beyond the tail. A deep flight call sounds like *frank.* Fish and eels form a major part of a heron's diet, though it may also take mice and small birds. They are swallowed whole, the indigestible portions being regurgitated as pellets.

For the heronry, deciduous trees are usual, but some birds select conifers – larch, spruce or pine. A heronry is a busy place from February, in the early part of which birds gather on boggy ground near the heronry and indulge in a pre-nesting ritual of neck-stretching and dancing, part of what my old friend Stan Lythe referred to as a getting-to-know-you routine.

Egg-laying on a flat platform of a nest takes place in early March. In calm weather, a strong smell of fish pervades the area and by April the occupied nests are apparent from the whitened state of the ground beneath some of the trees. Alas, all too often there are dead young birds which, being too venturesome, have tumbled from the nest. Stan Lythe, who photographed at a heronry, concluded that when young herons took their first flights, they must be able to find their way back to their own nest. It is only at the nest that food is provided for them.

The eggs are being incubated for about 25 days and the young are nestlings for from seven to eight weeks. Then the woodland resounds to a cacophony of strange sounds, including the clicking of mandibles. The chirping of tree sparrows, uninvited lodgers in the sides of the capacious nests, may also be heard.

Dipper

Cinclus cinclus

(one who studies the bird is a cinclologist)

Dales name: Water Ouzel.

This dumpy bird which looks black from a distance is really dark-brown and chestnut; there is a prominent white "bib". Notice how, when standing, the dipper frequently bobs. Simultaneously, a white nictitating membrane (inner eyelid) descends obliquely. The dipper's flight is fast and low and its flight call a metallic zit, zit, zit.

The dipper, our dale-country water sprite, resembles a wren in its general form and has a stumpy tail, though, unlike that of the wren, it is not elevated at an angle of 90 degrees. The dipper's world is the width of its chosen watercourse and the length of its territory, which might be no more than a few hundred yards. The bird bobs incessantly, a suggestion being that with a white breast it is less conspicuous against water breaking against stones.

This bird has a dual-purpose design, its wings being short and muscular, suitable both for flight and for propulsion underwater when feeding on the larvae of mayflies, caddis flies, stonefly and small fish. By exploiting the bed of a watercourse it has no serious rival and might remain in its territory the whole year through, unless there is a prolonged freeze-up in winter.

It is well equipped for its submarine excursions, which are most often seen in winter, when the water level is high. A dense plumage ensures it keeps warm. A prominent oil gland is available for waterproofing its feathers as it preens. This bird can close its nostril while under water. In summer, with the water level lower, the bird is content to dip its head only as it wades in the shallows. The most intense spells of feeding are at either end of the day.

A hungry dipper leaps into the water with a plop and "flies" against the current, being swaddled in silvery bubbles of air trapped in the feathers. More bubbles extend from the bird as it moves small pebbles to expose the creatures on which it feeds. Strong feet take a firm grip of the stream bed and assist it to grip and maintain a position against the flow. Sometimes the dipper walks into the water from the bank, with only its head beneath the surface. At other times, the bird runs down or drops from a midstream rock into the water, either submerging or floating on the current, its stubby wings unfurled.

The Dipper

Pair formation begins before the Old Year is out. Courtship is noticed as early as January or into February. The male's song is composed of scratchy notes and warbling trills, somewhat reminiscent of that of the common wren and at a pitch to allow it to be heard above the sound of the river. The domed nest is like a football composed of moss, with an entrance hole recessed below an upper lip. An inner cup is lined with dry leaves.

Bill Robson, surveying dipper nests on the northern Pennines, found that half of them were on rock faces, 16 per cent under bridges and 7 per cent under waterfalls. Some nests are used so often they are composed of living moss. He also deduced that a time lapse occurs between the nesting of lowland dippers and those on the high hills.

Generally, the first of the clutch, which averages five white eggs, is laid towards the end of March. The hen bird carries out the incubation. Both parents feed the young, which when the fledgling period is over appear to view clad in a greyish plumage. While waiting for a parent to bring food, a young dipper will bob on a stone or at the edge of a weir, its tail being cocked up like that of a wren.

Dippers are often double-brooded, with three or four young being reared each time. The birds are not conspicuous in late summer when they are in the moult and least prone to fly. They skulk quietly among the river or beckside vegetation and feed as they may.

Grey Wagtail

Motacilla cinerea

Dales name: Washtail.

A blue-grey mantle is off-set by a breast of lemon-yellow and there is a black gorget. The tail of this elegant wagtail is impressively long. The male is more colourful than the female but adults and young have a yellow flash at the sides and base of the tail. In winter, there is a southward dispersal, with a few crossing the Channel to sojourn on the Continent.

Where you find a dipper, it is more than likely you will also find a grey wagtail, which is a bird with a preference for fast-flowing upland streams. Watch this bird trip along the edge of a beck, constantly wagging its tail as it looks out for insect food, including flies, beetles and dragonflies. Insect food is also taken on the wing, especially over water.

Grey Wagtail

The grey wagtail's nest is usually made in derelict masonry or among tree roots on the face of a shadowy bank. Incubation and fledging are spread over about a month. A pair of grey wagtails may sometimes rear three broods in a season, though two is usual.

Kingfisher

Alcedo atthis

Dales name: Fisher

A flash of cobalt blue, low over a river or mill-dam, is usually all that marks the departure of a kingfisher, a bird with short wings and a short tail. Notice, if you have a sideways view, the dagger-like beak. The blue so obvious in the airborne kingfisher extends along its back and tail; otherwise the upperparts are emerald green. The underbody is a rich chestnut. The bird is white at the throat and sides of the neck.

The kingfisher, which has been romantically described as a living rainbow, frequents slow-flowing waters. Here are the minnows that form its principle food. Here, too, are the steep sandy banks where a pair of birds excavate a burrow leading into a nesting chamber.

Isolated from its surroundings, the kingfisher is the brightest object in view, yet this bird is not obvious when perched among vegetation at the riverside. When hunting, the kingfisher most often plunges into the water from a perch. Alternatively, it will hover on rapidly-beating wings above its own rainbow reflection before diving into the water.

The male bird offers a fish to the female prior to mating, which occurs (in the words of one human observer) amid "a whirr of vivid blue wings." The young appear to view in about the beginning of May, when they are over three weeks old. Their plumage is somewhat dull as compared with that of their parent. Before a fish is offered to a young bird, it is battered against a handy object like a tree root and care is taken to present the fish head-first.

Kingfishers are usually double-brooded. For the second brood, another burrow will be made.

Oystercatcher

Haematopus ostralegus

Common name: Sea pie

The oystercatcher is big, brash and conspicuous. Its pied plumage blends with the shingle beds of the upper dales but not with the emerald green of meadowland where most pairs now nest. Notice the long orange-red beak and the pink legs. A disturbed oystercatcher has an echo-rousing call, "klee-eep, klee-eep", as it circles.

This is primarily a coastal species, but for over 50 years birds have bred in dale-country far removed from the sea. The oystercatcher exchanges a diet of cockles and mussels (not oysters) for worms and other grassland creatures between mid-February and mid-August, when it returns to the coast.

Nesting may begin in late April but frequently, where shingle beds are being used, is retarded by heavy rain, leading to boistrous rivers. Oystercatchers have a curious mating "dance". The birds, assuming a hunched appearance, run towards each other with their bright bills pointing downwards and with clamorous calls. The hunched posture is adopted by a bird which is slinking away from its nest, a shallow scrape. The young hatch in early May and, clad in fluffy dark grey and white down, are soon active. Like all waders, they "freeze" and are inconspicuous when they hear the warning cries of their parents.

Some pairs of oystercatchers nest beside reservoirs, though with variations in the depth of the water by no means all are successful.

Mallard

Anas platyrhynchos

Dales name: Wild duck

A drake mallard in spring is a dandy. The bottle-green head is separated from the maroon breast by a neat white "collar". The plumage of the duck is basically a mixture of browns, offering cryptic coloration when she incubates her eggs at a nest set on the ground among vegetation. Notice its legs are set well back on its body. This bird waddles. In late summer and early autumn, when in eclipse (moult), a flightless period, the drake has a general resemblance to the duck.

The largest of the dabbling ducks, a mallard has a broad and flattened beak well-suited to filtering from the water small plant and animal matter. In the wild, the mallard is a cautious bird which "flights" to its feeding areas at dusk.

Large numbers of mallard in built-up areas subsist on park lakes and becksides largely on food thrown to them by kindly folk. When roosting beside water, these urban ducks are indifferent to the human presence, while showing some of their wild spirit on the appearance of a dog.

At the approach of the nesting season there tends to be a preponderance of drakes, leading to exacting times for ducks. It is not unusual to see several drakes in aerial pursuit of a frantic duck. Cross-breeding with domestic strains of duck, such as the Aylesbury, has led to some striking variations of plumage.

Dales farmers with wet spots on their land used to encourage mallard because they dined on snails, hosts to the dreaded liver-fluke in sheep.

Waterhen

Gallinula chloropus

Also known as the Moorhen (or merehen)

Once a common nesting species in the Dales, the waterhen has suffered badly from the depredations of feral mink. The plumage is mostly brownish black, which in bright light shines with blue and purple. A white line extends along the flanks. The red beak has a yellow tip. A shy bird, skulking in cover, the waterhen has a jerky manner when walking or swimming. The head is nodding and the tail flicking. The prominent white under-tail has a central dark stripe.

A moorhen looks clumsy in the air. Pitching down where there is cover, it soon jerks its way out of sight. When taken by surprise, the bird dives and remains submerged, with only its red and yellow beak to be seen above the water.

The waterhen feeds mainly on vegetable matter but it also consumes worms, slugs, snails and tadpoles. The nest is a waterside platform made of rushes, reeds, sedges and iris-flags, where available. Bill Robson, the Eden Valley naturalist, told me of a nest made of corrugated cardboard that toned with the eggs.

The fluffy black young have baldish pates suffused with a rich blue for a few days. Six or seven weeks elapse before they can fly and become independent of their parents.

Goosander

Mergus merganser

Dales name: None known.

Big and strong, the goosander has a rapid flight and more than holds its own in a turbulent river. In its breeding plumage, the drake has a dark green head and a gleaming pinky-white body. The female's head is brown and the body greyish.

This species is one of the "sawbills", so called because of serrated cutting edges to their bills, a means of retaining a hold on slippery fish. A moderately large water bird, the goosander has spread to Dales rivers in recent times. Anglers detest it because of its fondness for young trout and salmon. The nest is usually in a hollow tree from which the flightless ducklings tumble early in life, to be conducted to the nearest open water.

The other sawbill to be seen in the Dales is the **red-breasted merganser** *(Murgus serrator)*. The drake has a green head and reddish-brown breast, the female being brownish. A distinguishing feature between the two species is the merganser's double headcrest.

Sand Martin

Riparia riparia

Dales Name: Pit Martin

A visitor for nesting, arriving in late March from a wintering haunt on the southern edge of the Sahara, this small, slim bird is found where there are sandy banks near water. The bird's back and a breast-band are brown; the underparts white.

The burrows of sand martins end in cup-shaped nesting chambers where the eggs and subsequently the young repose on beds of straw and other vegetation, lined with feathers. The eggs, being in constant darkness, are white.

When nesting by a river, the sand martin runs the risk of losing its nesting burrow, washed out by a freshet. The bird persists. Most pairs are double-brooded.

Sandpiper

Riparia riparia

Dales name: Summer Snipe

Listen for a clear, tittering call – hee-dee-dee. Look for a slim and restless waterside bird, brownish-grey above, white on the underparts. It blends with water-washed stones. The sandpiper lets off surplus nervous energy by constant teetering (bobbing of its rear end). A white wing bar is conspicuous when the bird is in flight. At times the wings seem to vibrate like a tuning fork.

"Summer snipe" is a good name for the sandpiper, for the species is late to arrive for nesting, being first seen towards the end of April. It has a relatively short stay. In the Dales, sandpipers appear to shun stretches of beck or river where the fall is greater than 200 feet a mile. They also nest beside tarns and reservoirs.

The titter of the sandpiper is one of the lively aspects of a Dales spring. Notice how the bird keeps close to the water. The wingbeats are shallow and alternate with short spells of gliding. The song is "kitti-weewit, kitti-weewit, kitti-weewit." Nests have been found on shingle, but usually are well-concealed.

It is believed that a female sandpiper produces several distinct clutches of eggs and leaves it to paternal males to hatch them out. Thus does this summer visitor to the Dales make the most of what is a relatively short season. In August, most of our breeding birds start out on a long journey to Africa, some going as far as Cape Province and Madagascar.

Canada Goose

Branta canadensis.

Dales name: None is known.

A bird introduced to this country in the 17th century to adorn parkland lakes is now, in a feral state, extremely common. Look for a tall goose with a black head, a long black neck and white chin-patch. The body is brown. The call is a trumpet-like honking.

The Canada goose was known as a domestic bird in Britain by 1678 and in the 18th century was breeding in the grounds of large estates. Feral groups were being noticed by the mid-19th century, and by the end of the century it was present in northern England.

It has become well-established on rivers, reservoirs, gravel pits and marshes. Many pairs nest on the moors and conduct their offspring to the nearest large stretch of water, such as Stocks reservoir (Hodder Valley) and Gouthwaite (Nidderdale). Up to 500 geese are to be found in the Stocks area. To listen to the calls of those commuting to and from the Ribble Valley is a memorable experience in winter.

Great Crested Grebe

Podiceps cristatus

Dales name: None.

This large water bird is to be seen on many inland waters. The great-crested grebe in winter is unimpressive. Hump-backed, floating low in the water, it offers for view a slim neck, thin head and slender bill. The breast, foreneck and face are white. The bird is transformed in the nesting season when it assumes black ear tufts and a chestnut ruff tipped with black. Notice the broad white wing bars on rapidly-beating wings when, as occasionally happens, the grebe takes flight.

The spring display of grebes in their exotic nuptial plumage brings to the lakes and reservoirs of the Dales a touch of Oriental splendour. Being similar in appearance, each plays a part in a complicated rite which leads to pair-bonding. The ordinary display involves head-shaking. A pair does this in concert, taking turns, sometimes quickly, sometimes slowly, as they face each other with upraised ear tufts and ruffs.

Then there is the "penguin dance". As performed by great-crested grebes, it might almost be part of some pre-nuptial ballet. One grebe holds its head low in a threat posture. The other grebe approaches with a similar gesture. The heads are raised, the birds meet chest to chest, with thin necks extended. Heads waggle and frills expand to the accompaniment of discordant clacking notes.

The grebes now make abortive stabs at the back feathers. They lower their heads and swim apart, until some 30 yards separate them. The birds dive, re-surface close to each other, each with a beakful of weed. Face to face they raise themselves vertically and offer each other the weed. For a few seconds, only the rump and feet of each bird touch the water and their bodies and necks are held rigidly vertical. Their ardour then subsides, the weeds are dropped and a former languid manner resumed.

The nest is a substantial but loose collection of aquatic plants. Usually it floats, being tethered either to water plants or to a tree branch with twigs at water level. Nesting at reservoirs is chancy because of the tendency for the water level to fluctuate considerably. Young grebes, which are zebra-striped, have the ability to swim immediately and while small ride on the backs of their parents.

Black-headed Gull

Larus ridibundus

Dales Name: Black Cap Gull

In summer, dark brown cap. In winter, just a smudge behind the eye. This is the only species of gull frequenting the Dales which has red legs. The bird has an unlovely rasping call.

Most black-headed gulls nest inland. In the Dales, colonies are to be found by moorland tarns. The once big gullery high on Whernside is no more, but black-headed gulls nest densely on an island in Stocks Reservoir and can be watched (and most certainly heard) from the eastern shore where the road is flanked by moderately high walls.

SCRUB AND WOODLAND

With less than one per cent of the landscape under timber, the Dales are the least wooded of the National Parks of England and Wales. The remnants of ash woodland occur on the sides of the upper valleys and in gills. In most cases, the browsing of sheep prevents the natural regeneration of timber. Large areas of the Dales are now clogged by conifer plantations.

Common Buzzard

Buteo buteo

Dales Name: Glead or Gled

The buzzard rides a thermal, high above the ground, circling languidly with its wings curling upwards at the tips. The short, outspread tail helps the bird to trim itself to the updraught from a cliff or ridge. The general tone is brown but notice the paler patches beneath the wings. The mewing call – "whee-u" – enlivens craggy areas and woodland settings alike. The buzzard occasionally perches on telegraph poles, when it assumes a hunched appearance. The bird is not fussy over its food and tackles most items from worms to carrion.

Arthur Brook described the buzzard, a relic of the old Dales avifauna, as a sheep in wolf's clothing. "He apes the eagle in appearance and is in fact a clumsy coward." Not so. The buzzard, which is spreading back to its old Dales haunts, is a skilful hunter as well as a carrion-eater. The bird is also a supreme aeronaut, soaring gracefully on a thermal with no more effort than flexing its pinion jaunts.

The fact that the buzzard has survived great changes in the landscape and attitude to birds with hooked beaks speaks well for its staying power. A low point was reached in 1953-4, when myxomatosis decimated the rabbit population (which has since recovered). Some gamekeepers believe the presence of buzzards does more good than harm. If a buzzard is riding a thermal, in August or September, when there are lots of pheasants, these birds recognise it as a bird of prey and do not stray out of the woods.

For a time, the buzzard's last refuge was on the Howgill Fells of the north-west but a "spread" is in progress, involving the wooded areas of the Yorkshire-Lancashire border country and the eastern dales. The buzzard might be seen on the wind at the head of Wensleydale. One of a pair regularly seen in a North Craven wood is wearing jesses, so a falconer's buzzard is consorting with a thoroughly wild bird. Buzzards have an exciting courtship ritual. A male bird circles just above a female and, sometimes, dives wildly past her before swooping up again. A buzzard is sometimes content to collect food by descending on a small mammal from a perch on a tree. A pair of birds in the upper Lune valley fed their young entirely on frogs.

It is the custom of the buzzard to embellish its nest with sprigs of greenery plucked from rowan or thorn. Laying takes place towards the end of April. A young buzzard close to flight has a quaint beauty. The rich, dark brown plumage is offset at the head by a fuzz of grey down, giving the impression it has donned a knitted helmet. When the youngster opens its beak, for food or to give a ringing call, a red gape is revealed. Last year's young are distinguished by the white tips to their tails.

The legs of rough-legged buzzards are feathered down to the toes. Birds arrive in eastern Yorkshire from the tundra and forest regions of Scandinavia. The species is regularly seen at Gouthwaite, in Upper Nidderdale, where it may be distinguished from the common buzzard by a larger, paler form, especially about the head, though variations do occur in common buzzard, with possible confusion between species.

The rough-leg has a white-base to the tail and a black band at the head. This species tends to hover in search of prey.

Tawny Owl

Strix aluco.

Dales name: Hoot Owl.

The male bird gives "the edge o' dark" some drama with its "hoo-hoo-hoo" call. It does not say "to-whit-to-wooo." The female's calls are less dramatic. Both give a distinctive "ke-wick" that cuts cleanly through the night air.

If you are fortunate to see a tawny owl at its daytime roost, on a branch where it joins the tree, notice its tawny-brown plumage, a range of tones not unlike those of the woodland haunts. The eyes are like big black grapes.

The tawny owl, a bird of mature woodland, has a look-out perch where it awaits the near presence of prey. The owl's soft plumage ensures a silent approach to any small mammal scuttering below. One of the more unusual prey items seen in the Dales was a treecreeper, plucked from a depression on a tree where the bird had been roosting.

When the eggs are due to hatch, a tawny owl tends to store prey as spare food at the nest. Sometimes, you may come across some of the downy young out of the nesting hole. Their soft grey down makes then inconspicuous unless they have perched on a wall or fencing posts. Leave them alone or a watchful female, at her nearby perch, may attack you - from behind.

Willow Warbler

Phylloscopus trochilus

Known in some areas of the Dales as featherpoke.

This delicate-looking bird, denizen of woodland edge and scrubland, has migrated all the way from the tropics for nesting. The bird is olive-green above with whitish underparts. There is a prominent "eye-brow". The song, brief and delicate, is on a descending scale.

Chiff Chaff

Phylloscopus collybita

A somewhat similar warbler, but a true woodland bird, the song is unmistakable, being a repeated chiff-chaff-chiff-chaff.

Wood Warbler

Phylloscopus sibilatrix

also known in the Dales as wood wren.

The largest of the leaf-warblers, and also a true woodlander, this warbler, which returns to the Dales in May, has a greenish back, yellow throat and upper breast, the underparts being otherwise white. Listen for the call – a protracted whistle – and a song that is rendered in two parts. The first is a trill and the second a succession of its call-notes.

Goldcrest

Regulus regulus

Dales name: None known

A diminutive bird, it is seen mainly in coniferous woodland. Notice the olive-green form, short wings and tail, needle-thin bill and a golden "crown", edged with black. The crown of the male bird has a touch of orange. Listen for a thin, high-pitched call – "see-see-see". The song has been likened to the sound of a fairy's sewing-machine

The goldcrest tends to feed at high level but if a close sighting is possible the bird does not seem to mind. Avoid a sudden movement. The breeding season begins towards the end of April and it is then that the male bird displays his colourful "crown" to the female. The nest is of the hammock type, being suspended under a branch. The materials used in its construction, which is mainly the work of the female, includes lichen and cobwebs.

Sparrowhawk

Accipiter nisus

Dales name: Blue hawk

This streamlined bird-catcher is slate-grey above, with pale cheeks and a light eyestripe. The underparts are whitish. There are brown bands on the tail. The sparrowhawk has especially large legs and talons, evolved to grasp birds on the wing. One pair studied in the Dales slew 15 different species of bird, from sparrow and house martin to great spotted woodpecker.

At nesting time, which begins quite late, in mid-May, a pair of sparrowhawks may use the old nest of another species, such as the carrion crow or, in a coniferous area, select a larch tree and nest at an elevation of from 12ft to 16ft. Four or five roundish eggs are laid. They hatch out in five weeks and another three weeks or more ensues before the young birds are capable of flight.

During this time, the male bird kills small birds, takes them to a plucking area, then calls the female off the nest to collect the prey and pass it to the young. The plucking area and the nest take on the appearance of a butcher's shop as the season progresses. A pair of hawks in Gisburn Forest were collecting whinchats from the high ground round about.

Though it is a hawk of the forest edge, or an area with scattered trees, the sparrowhawk is also likely to be seen in leafy suburbs, where, deceived by through lounges in modern houses, it has been known to stun or kill itself by colliding with plate glass.

Green Woodpecker

Picus viridis

Dales name: Yaffle

If you are fortunate to see the green woodpecker, notice the bright red crown, a red moustache (male), green back and yellow-green rump. This is a comparatively large, heavy woodpecker, a resident of park-like countryside and fellside woods. It is more often heard than seen. The name yaffle comes from its laughing cry

The green woodpecker may be seen perched on the ground as well as in a tree. It has a partiality for ants. Unlike the spotted woodpeckers, it does not habitually use the resonance of a dead branch as a drum. Its laughing cry is a noisy feature of spring and one bird might be heard responding to the call of another. It flies with a bounding action, keeping quite low.

The nest is a tree-hole, a typical example being a neat hole driven into the underside of a sloping branch. The adults, when feeding young, have a shuttle service, arriving at the nest in intervals of about an hour. The rasping of woodpecker claws on the trunk alerts and activates the young. A churring sound is heard from the nesting hole – a sound maintained until the feeding session is over. The woodpecker jerks up its head, regurgitating food into the bill of the nearest youngster. The adult may partly enter the nesting hole, only the yellow rump and tail remaining in view.

Tree-creeper

Certhia familiaris

Dales name: None recorded

The tree-creeper is mouse-like as it scurries up the trunk of a tree, stopping to probe cracks and crannies for food. Its decurved beak looks as fine as a needle. The upperparts of the bird are patterned with brown and black. As it flies to the base of the next tree, the silvery underparts are revealed. In its upward progress, the bird uses its large claws for clinging and a long stiffened tail as a prop. In flight, the tail is seen to have two points.

In winter, a tree-creeper might be seen in the company of a mixed flock of titmice. Its food includes beetles, wood lice, spiders and their eggs. The male bird's song, heard as early as February, is high-pitched and not easy to distinguish. It begins with a single phrase and, after a pause, ends with a flourish of notes.

The tree-creeper's nest is usually behind some loose bark. Birds have been found roosting in saucer-shaped hollows made in the thick and friable bark of the Wellingtonia *(Sequoia gigantea).*

Nuthatch

Sitta europaea

Dales name: Kenspekle

Look for a bird which, clinging to the trunk of a tree, shows a blue-grey crown and mantle. The underparts are a sandy-brown, the throat being white. This bird is equally adroit when moving up or down the tree.

The nuthatch is sedentary and, in a grim winter, relies greatly on the food put out on bird tables by householders living in well-timbered areas. Normally, it frequents mature deciduous trees, such as in Strid Wood at Bolton Abbey. A portly bird with a stubby tail and straight bill, the nuthatch explores cracks and crannies for food. Its name is believed to derive from *nut-hack,* a reference to the bird's habit of ramming a nut in a crevice on the bark of a tree and hacking the nut to remove the shell.

The nuthatch has a loud, clear, errand-boy type of whistle. The song is a repetition at speed of *quilp-quilp.* Courtship displays in late March or April include a pursuit on the trunk and branches of a tree. The nest is situated in a hole, the size of the entrance being adapted by plastering it up with mud until the aperture is of a suitable size for use by the bird.

Woodcock

Scolopax rusticola

Dales Name: None recorded

A Dales poacher was said to be able to detect a bird sitting on a woodland floor by the sparkle in one of its eyes, the plumage being cryptic, harmonising with leaf-litter. In spring, a slow display flight (roding) is watchable at dawn and dusk. The bird is revealed as a stout, long billed bird with rounded wings and a distinctive call, repeated at intervals, and described to me long years ago by Paul Holmes of the Malham Tarn Field Centre as "three grunts and a squeak".

The woodcock, a bird of the gloaming, was familiar to me during the years I conducted field studies of sika deer in and around the Ribble Valley. I was in an area of small estates where woodland, which contained some oak, was carefully managed and the trees "brashed" to provide growing space. I would very occasionally locate a woodcock on a carpet of leaves in a dry part of a wood. The nest is a depression on the ground where it will sit hard when an intruder is close. It is best not to press such a bird which, when the intruder has gone, is inclined to desert a nest with eggs.

The bird feeds at intervals from dusk to dawn, flying to a familiar boggy area and probing with a long bill for succulent worms and other items of food. The beak having nerves, the bird is able to locate food, assess it and swallow it without actually seeing what it has eaten. The woodcock misses little. The eyes are so placed that this bird has a good backward vision. The ears are below the front edges of the eyes and, therefore, when the bird is probing for food, are close to the earth.

The woodcock is an early nester. A brooding bird sits through the storms of late March and the eggs hatch in early April. Arthur Gilpin was taking photographs from a hide in a Wharfedale wood as someone approached the area. The incubating woodcock lowered its head so that its long bill was pushed forward beneath the dead leaves and bluebell stems. The body was then flattened to the earth. "Apart from the eye, large and lustrous, the whole looked like another collection of fallen leaves." When the four eggs have hatched and the chicks dried off, the young birds are led from the nesting area. A woodcock chick, like its parents, tones perfectly with the ground.

Woodcock are not exclusively woodland birds. The author came across a pair with new-hatched young while following a path on a hill-side above Cotterdale, in Upper Wensleydale. One afternoon, on the moorland trod between Swinnergill and Old Gang above Swaledale, he was in the company of a local man, Matthew Cherry, when a wood-cock hurriedly gathered a chick between its thighs and, with difficulty, rose from heather near the track. The bird departed with cumbersome flight.

Redstart

Phoenicurus phoenicurus

Dales name: Wrenny red-tail

The crown and mantle of this summer visitor to old woodland is grey and the breast is tinted orange. Notice also a white forehead, black cheeks and throat. The bird's most conspicuous feature is a quivering tail, which is bright red. The call is a lively hwee-tuk-tuk.

Look for the redstart in the sunshine, not the shade of the woodland floor. It is present in quite small tracts of woodland and in wooded gills. It feed on tit-bits collected from tree trunks and leaves.

Pheasant

Phasianus colchicus

Dales name: Nothing truly local

The male is a bobby-dazzler, with a green head, a red face and wattles. A white neck signifies the bird's ancestors lived in China. The female has a brown plumage, needing to be drab as camouflage when on the nest. Feral pheasants nest widely. The majority of the birds reared for sport are now obtained as poults from hatcheries. The call of the pheasant is a harsh crowing. Flush a bird and it takes to the air with a cackling sound.

The Pheasant, a common game-bird

For long classified as a game-bird, the pheasant escapes land-based predators like the fox by roosting in trees At the mating season, cock pheasants which nest in the wild will battle it out for the favours of the hens. You can always tell when a pheasant, having the company of females, has been "treading" hard, because he loses a portion of his tail feathers.

The pheasant is not the best of mothers. She sits tightly on her eggs under brambles or dead bracken, while the cock bird struts about on his territory, his red wattles meeting together on the top of his head. When hatched, the female leads off her chicks. Any chick that does not manage to keep up with her is usually left behind.

BUILDINGS

The farming revolution in remoter dales has resulted in the presence of many derelict buildings, including redundant field barns and small farmsteads where land has been amalgamated to form larger, viable units. No buildings should be entered without the permission of the farmer or landowner. It should be possible to watch bird traffic from a nearby footpath. A barn in North Craven holds many pairs of jackdaws. Nearly every barn has its starling nest. Stock doves, which are shy little birds, nest in buildings in remote settings.

Swallow

Hirundo rustica

Dales name: None recorded.

The swallow, the most familiar of the summer bird visitors, is steely-blue above, with a blue breast band. The underparts are cream to orange-buff. Notice the chestnut patch on the forehead and chin. The swallow has long swept-back wings and conspicuous tail-streamers that are longest in the male bird. A lively twittering call is heard in flight or when birds perch on overhead cables and wires.

The swallow usually arrives in the dale-country in April. A harrowing migratory journey involves crossing the Sahara from wintering areas in Africa. The presence of outbuildings at hill farms has permitted swallows to nest at about 1,000ft/300m. The males are thought to have the strongest allegiance to a nesting area and pair with females on arrival. In some cases, pairs occupy the same sites, though with high mortality on migration, new partners must be frequently necessary.

The nest, a cup of mud and grass, lined with feathers, is usually supported underneath and is made against a wall, ensuring a firm situation. Making the nest occupies the breeding pair for between eight and 10 days. The clutch of eggs, from three to six, are incubated for about 14 days and young swallows remain in the nest for around 21 days. Most pairs of swallows are double-brooded. A few manage to raise three broods.

House Martin

Delichon urbica

Dales name: Eaves Swallow.

Though superficially like a swallow, the differences are soon noticeable. The house martin is dark blue above, all-white underneath and has a broad white patch between back and tail which shows up prominently in flight, especially in poor light. The house martin has shorter wings than the swallow and its forked tail has no streamers. The martin builds its mud nest on the outside of a building, under the eaves or in a top corner of a window.

Before buildings were commonplace, house martins would plaster their mud nests to overhangs on cliffs, as at Malham Cove and Kilnsey Crag. In the Craven district, where barns have impressive porches, it is not unusual to find a colony of house martins nesting against the rafters.

Among the most elevated nests in the Dales are those at stations on the Settle-Carlisle railway, the highest station being Dent, where the old Stationmaster's House, at 1,150ft/345m, is regularly used. The most durable recorded nest was surely one at a Pennine farm where the yard was being concreted and the birds helped themselves to the cement.

Barn Owl

Tyto alba

Dales name: Screech Owl

The now-rare barn owl has golden-buff upperparts that are mottled with grey. The heart-shaped face and underparts are white. When it flies at dusk, it is like a big white moth.

The nesting season begins quite late and is prolonged. Eggs are laid towards the end of May and incubation beings as soon as an egg is laid. An owl family therefore consists of youngsters of various sizes. They have a long fledging period – some 10 weeks – and are in lusty growth when the countryside teems with small mammals.

Each owlet will eat one or two rodents daily, so the demand for food to cater for a family of up to five is considerable. The prey is swallowed whole and the indigestible parts are regurgitated as shiny black pellets. At nesting time the young birds "snore" and hiss to stimulate the parents to go food-hunting.

Swift

Apus apus

Dales name: Dicky Devilling

The head, cigar-shaped body and scimitar-shaped wings are of such a dark shade of brown they appear black when seen against the brightness of the sky. The tail is short and forked. A swift utters a piercing scream in flight. A chorus of screams is heard as parties of birds speed low over the roofs of a town or village.

This bird spends almost all its life on the wing. It is weatherwise and at the approach of a thunderstorm might fly a vast distance to avoid it. The narrow wings, which cut cleanly through the air, are held stiffly out when gliding and are stiffly held when being beaten at speed.

The nest is tucked in holes under roofs. This bird cannot perch but must cling to masonry. In unseasonably cold weather, the swift has the ability to become torpid for a while, a break in the otherwise constant search for food.

Though urban-based, the swift is a familiar sight to anyone who climbs the high hills in the Dales, where it pursues insect life. It is a surprise to those who have ascended to the plateau of Ingleborough, over 2,000ft/600m above sea level, to see swifts in the air. When feeding, a swift can open its bill almost to the full width of its head to catch the insects on which it preys for food.

Kestrel

Falco tinnunculus

Dales name: Windhover

The kestrel, a relatively small bird of prey, hovers at a height of about 50ft/15m over likely areas and makes a steep dive on to the voles which are its favourite food. This bird has a wide range of habitats, being seen at the side of motorways and on remote fellsides. Distinguishing features are a grey head, a black "moustache", chestnut back and light underparts. The kestrel seeks voles and any other palatable item that comes its way.

The kestrel is our commonest bird of prey. As it hovers, while questing for food, the wings flap steadily as the bird fixes its bright eyes on the ground beneath. The kestrel makes no proper nest. It is catholic in its choice of site. Some pairs nest in crannies on cliffs. Others select the old nest of a pair of crows or pigeons. In areas of redundant buildings, kestrels have been found nesting in alcoves over the door or in gaps in walls.

A nest in the wall of an old farmhouse on the catchment of Stocks Reservoir was high on the gable end of the building but could be scrutinised at close quarters by anyone who walked (with care) into a former bedroom.

Incubation of the eggs extends over about 28 days and the young fly in about the same length of time.

BIRD WATCHING IN WINTER

Whooper Swan

Northern Swans

Autumn brings whooper swans from Iceland and Bewick's swans from the Arctic tundra. They are not as widespread as they were now that thousands of these northern swans are attracted by regular food and sanctuary to refuges just north of Solway and at Martin Mere in Lancashire. Icelandic swans tackle the arduous 500-mile journey to Britain and given good weather conditions will make their first landfall in about 12 hours. Mostly, the bird stays close to the sea though swans have been recorded at considerable heights. Unlike the mute swan, which is with us the year round, the whooper is conversational. It utters bugle-like notes.

The whooper swan *(Cygnus cygnus)* holds its neck straight when swimming (the mute swans neck is usually curved). The beak is black-and-yellow. Bewick's swan *(Cygnus bewickii)* is in effect a smaller version of the whooper, having a shorter neck and less yellow on its beak. The voice of Bewick's Swan is higher pitched, being almost like the yapping of a terrier.

Bewick's swans nest to the east of the Taymyr in northern Siberia. The journey to wintering haunts in England might take two months, with stops at long familiar staging posts on the Continent.

A Conspicuous Duck

Goldeneye from Scandinavia and western Russia dive for food and are seldom seen on land. Notice also the triangular head and short bill. The male is white, with a black head and a large white spot between the eye and the bill. The female, in comparison, looks dark. A record number of 26 goldeneye have been recorded on Malham Tarn towards the end of winter, when the males might display a touch of spring fever. They tip back their heads, touching their backs, then stretch up their necks and simultaneously kick their legs, making the water cream with their splashing. The goldeneye flies swiftly and the beat of the wings produces a musical whistling. A few pairs nest in Cumbria.

"Snow" Thrushes

Appreciable numbers of fieldfares and redwings from Scandinavia and northern Europe arrive in this country in October and the first arrivals tend to linger in hill country like the Dales, stripping the thorn and rowan trees of their scarlet berries. Fieldfare flocks seen in November contain a good number of juveniles.

Redwings

The fieldfare's chacking call is heard as straggling flocks of birds cross a frost-stiffened landscape. The redwing utters sibilant calls at night as parties migrate. A fieldfare is a large thrush which looks as though it has been patched with grey. This tone is seen on head and rump, the mantle and wings having a chestnut hue. The redwing, which is the smallest of the European thrushes, has a white eye stripe to aid identity, and takes its name from patches of chestnut-red on the underwing and flanks which are best seen when the bird is in flight.

WHERE TO WATCH THE BIRDS

Use the Ordnance Survey Outdoor Leisure maps of the Yorkshire Dales, 1:25 000, for precise details of access to the areas mentioned and for hatched green lines which indicate footpaths. The most practical book is *Where to Watch Birds in Yorkshire,* by John R Mather, published by Christopher Helm/A & C Black.

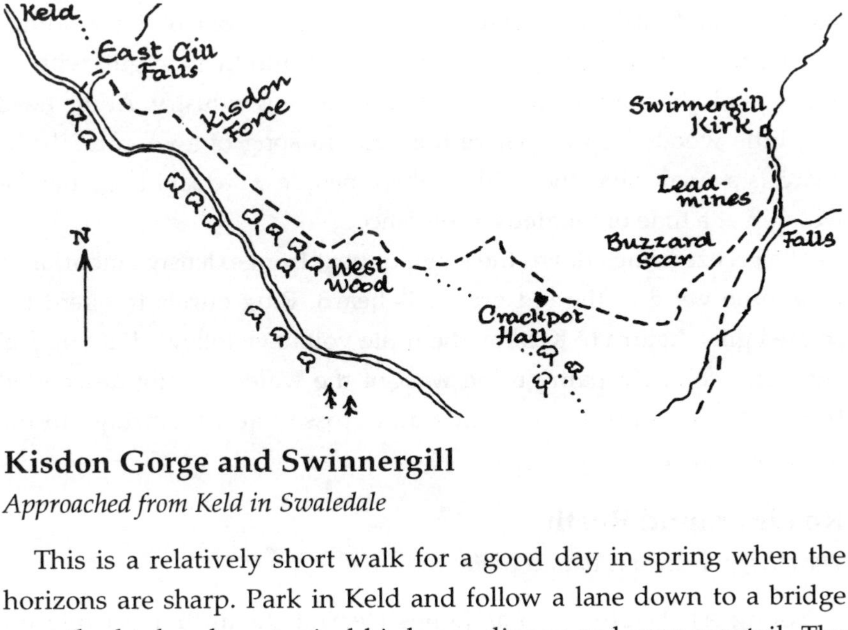

Kisdon Gorge and Swinnergill

Approached from Keld in Swaledale

This is a relatively short walk for a good day in spring when the horizons are sharp. Park in Keld and follow a lane down to a bridge over the beck, where typical birds are dipper and grey wagtail. The bridge is well-used, for it is crossed by the stretch of Pennine Way between Thwaite and Tan Hill, where stands the highest licensed premises in England, 1,732ft/528m. Those walking Mr Wainwright's Coast to Coast Walk use the bridge, bearing right (as we shall do) on a high-lying path which climbs above West Wood on its way to Swinnergill.

Kisdon Hill, 1,640ft/499m, dominates the landscape to your right. Its name is Celtic and means "small detached hill". Thatched by ling, the hill is tenanted by red grouse. Birds to look out for on the walk are lapwing, skylark and wheatear. You may even hear the chatter of the peregrine and a familiar springtime sound is the bubbling call of the curlew. In winter, the sight of a raven is a possibility. Young ravens from the northern fells tend to drift into the Dales.

The track passes Crackpot, now sadly ruined. The name Crackpot is said to mean "a cave frequented by crows". Inside one of the buildings are the remains of a smithy. The path turns into Swinnergill, with its gaunt reminders of the once mighty lead-mining industry. At the head of a little wooded gorge where the strident song of a wren might be heard is a small cave, the "kirk", where people were said to gather for worship at a time of religious intolerance.

The breeze brings down the smell of peat from extensive moorlands where the voice of the red grouse is heard. Ring ouzels frequent the shaded gills. Return to Keld by the route you have followed. If you feel energetic, follow a path on the west of the water, having descended from Swinnergill to the riverside and crossed at a footbridge to the north of Muker.

Roads around Reeth

The village of Reeth is in Swaledale

Young Alf Wight, who as James Herriot the author became the world's best-known vet, dated his romance with the Yorkshire Dales from the day when, on his rounds, he stopped beside a moorland road above Reeth. Looking down the dale towards Richmond, his senses were overwhelmed by the beauty of the valley, its flanking woods and moors.

Three Water Birds

Above: Teal, breeds near Grimwith and Gouthwaite and high moorland haunts. *Left:* Wigeon, a winter visitor to the Ribble Valley, Malham Tarn and Semerwater. *Below:* Canada goose, a common species on inland waters, with over 400 in the vicinity of Stocks Reservoir.

The moors are picturesque in late summer, when the bonnie heather blooms. Birdwise, they are at their best in springtime, when the resident grouse have been joined, for nesting, by such upland waders as golden plover, curlew, lapwing and redshank. Any number of unfenced roads that are worth following cross the moorland. From the higher stretches of road, you look across a succession of bare ridges and marvel that so much open and under-used land exists in this "tight little island".

Use the car as a "hide" and, being prepared to do more than glance, you may see some birds at relatively close quarters. Especially grouse, which are in their territories as early as November and stir the echoes with their crowing in March and April.

A direct road from Reeth to Leyburn runs along the edge of an Army range, where the tousled vegetation holds a goodly number of birds. Try to avoid mid-afternoon, when bird life is languid. Morning and evening are the periods when grouse and other moorland birds become active and noisy. Southwards from Grinton, roads head for Wensleydale, meeting the dale at Redmire and Askrigg. From Reeth, motor up Swaledale to Low Row and cross to Langthwaite in Arkengarthdale. Or go down-dale to Fremington and, just beyond, on the road to Marske, turning left along a cul de sac to the old lead mining area of Hurst.

Howgill Fells

Approached from Sedbergh

Cautley Spout, which is clearly visible from the vicinity of the Cross Keys beside the A683, is a series of falls, totalling 650ft/200m. A bridge crosses the Rawthey and a conspicuous footpath leads to the base of the Spout. Such is the grandeur of the scene that the Spout is much further away from the road than you might imagine.

Notice, as you walk, the huge dark face of Cautley Crag, the most

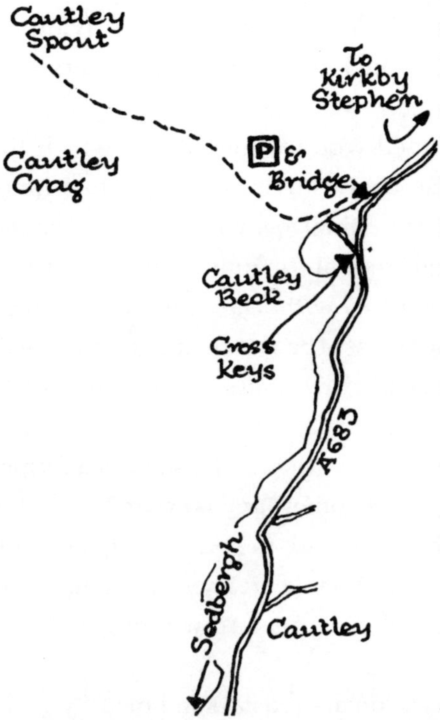

rugged scenery on a collection of rounded fells known as the Howgills. They are named after an obscure hamlet in the Lune Valley. The crag and the hollow below it were fashioned in the Ice Age when an enormous mass of ice cut back into the hill.

If you have the energy, climb the steep path beside the falls and walk on beside Force Gill Beck to the Calf, 2,200ft/676m, the highest point of the Howgills. Do not undertake the fell walk without durable clothing and, ideally, a map of the locality.

You would be unlucky in spring and summer not to see a raven, maybe even a peregrine and a buzzard, while the cheery voices of skylark and meadow pipit add to the bleating of sheep and infuse a sense of life to a bleak area. The meadow pipit has a "shuttlecock" display flight in spring, descending noisily, with wings and tail stiffened.

Ingleton Waterfalls

From Ingleton.

Two deep and rocky glens accommodate the Rivers Twiss and Doe, which blend their waters at Ingleton to form the Greta. The Glens Walk, of 4.5 miles/7.2km, begins and ends at Ingleton (A65). The route was opened up for visitors in 1885 and is served by a system of paths and walkways. An inexpensive leaflet about the Ingleton Waterfalls Trail, published by the Yorkshire Dales National Park, is available locally. The starting point (and paybox) are by the river. A large car park is available.

The walker first explores the well-wooded glen down which the Twiss flows from Kingsdale, then crosses over, through open limestone country, to return to Ingleton by the Doe, which drains Chapel-le-Dale. On the outward way, the trees are mainly deciduous and a series of splendid waterfalls culminates with Thornton Force, which roars out like a prophet in the wilderness. The return offers a change of mood, the path being in a gorge shaded by mature and more widely spaced trees, many of them being oak.

An early experience may be the clear *zit, zit* and the sight of a dipper flying arrow-like just above the river. Another familiar river bird is the grey wagtail. The *chwink* of the chaffinch and, in spring, ringing laugh of the green woodpecker and the two-syllable "rusty saw" song of the great tit are clearly heard in a glen which is so narrow it might almost be an echo chamber.

In the glens during the nesting season are redstart and pied flycatcher. The spring chorus includes the songs of willow warbler, chiff chaff, blackcap and garden warbler. The nuthatch finds an all-the-year-round haven here and in winter you may see a flock of assorted titmice and with tree-creeper in attendance.

A refreshment hut stands in an area where visitors once fed red squirrels and now have chaffinches and other birds in close attendance. At Thornton Force, the water pours 45ft/14m from a horizontal lip of Carboniferous limestone, below which is a bed of almost vertical Ordovician slates. The list of birds seen in this district include peregrine falcon, buzzard and raven. On the open ground are wheatear (rocks and drystone walls), also curlews and lapwings.

Ingleborough

Approached from Chapel-le-Dale

This is a 6 mile/10 km expedition to and from the summit plateau of the best-known hill in the Dales. Birds are thinly spread across the Three Peaks, as Ingleborough, Whernside and Penyghent are known, but good views of what exists are usually possible from the footpath. A boardwalk installed by English Nature extends over boggy ground and, for the stiff final climb, stones have been arranged in the form of steps. In wet weather the boardwalk and any limestone rock might be slippery.

Begin just to the north of Old Hill Inn, where there is space to park a car at the verge of the B6255. The steepest side of Ingleborough dominates the skyline. The route to be taken is clearly delineated. The hill achieved National Nature Reserve status, the area involved covering 991 hectares. Anyone who decides to ascend the hill is unlikely to lack human company. Alfred Wainwright, the guide book writer, commented: "Ingleborough…is probably the most ascended mountain in the country outside Lakeland." Alfred J Brown, a great walker in the 1930s, wrote: "Like most Yorkshiremen, I was taught in my boyhood to regard Ingleborough as a sort of Everest."

The first bird you are likely to see is a wheatear. This species chacks and whistles where there are drystone walls and rock outcrops. Some pairs nest in vacated rabbit burrows. In spring, the low fields of Chapel-le-Dale hold Swaledale ewes and their lambs. Cross the road to where a signpost marks the start of the footpath to Ingleborough, the distance given being 2 ³/₈ mile. As the walk begins, notice a well-preserved limekiln on the left and, to the right, a notice of welcome by English Nature to the Ingleborough reserve, which contains one of the country's finest tracts of limestone pavement.

Several stiles are negotiated in a walk across limestone pastures,

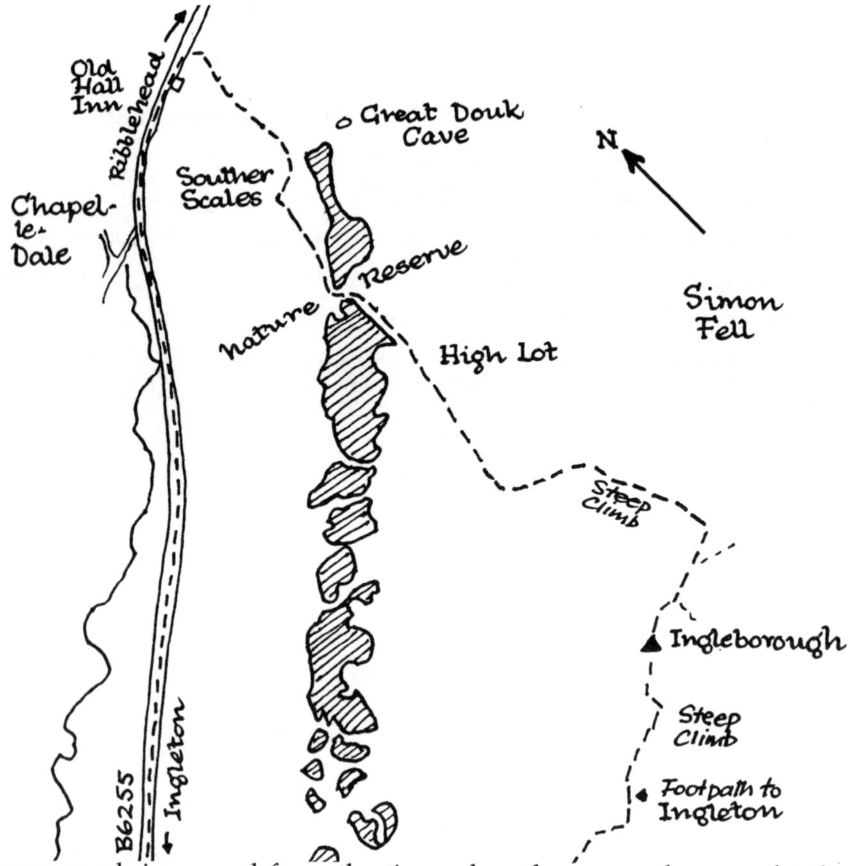

now much improved from the time when they were damp and tufty enough to attract nesting lapwings, which are to be found on the skirts of the great hill. In spring, the skylark is in jubilant song. The path climbs gently to the level of the pavement, which is crossed at Southerscales, a reserve owned by Yorkshire Wildlife Trust. More wheatears will be seen. In April, you might hear the cock bird's creaky little song. The path runs close to what is claimed to be the largest shakehole in the region. A pair of ring ouzels has been known to nest here.

Using one of two available stiles, enter High Lot, where the boardwalk makes walking easier while not sparing the walker the ascent. Here the commonest bird is the meadow pipit, with a friendly chirruping call and a display flight in which it turns itself into a shuttlecock, descending with stiffened wings and tail feathers, singing all the while. High Lot, like so much land in the Dales, has suffered from having too many sheep and little heather remains. You may, however, see a red grouse and you will undoubtedly hear, if not see, a curlew, and maybe observe a short-eared owl.

Ingleborough now appears to blot out three-quarters of the sky. The steep climb to the ridge near the summit is intimidating but well within a normal person's ability providing the ascent is not rushed. Take special care in wet weather. At the top, notice there are large areas of peat and heather – a type of landscape, which suits the golden plover, though only one or maybe two pairs nest on the hill. In August, a moderately large number of birds converge on soft ground near Sulber Nick, on the Ribblesdale side, to join the lapwings in feeding on invertebrates such as leather jackets.

More stone steps raise the visitor to the level of the plateau, where a windbreak with seats is welcome; the central feature is an indicator of natural features to be viewed. The trig. point of the Ordnance Survey is no longer used but might be patted as a mark of achievement. The Rev John Hutton, who ascended Ingleborough around 1780, summed up the experience of the many who have climbed the hill since. He wrote: "Though we had many a weary and slippery step, we thought ourselves amply repaid when we got to the top, with the amusement we received on viewing the several extensive and diversified prospects."

In summer, a raven family might be seen on Ingleborough. The author saw a party of summering ravens playing with a cast-off plastic bag. A bird-watcher has a bonus in spring on encountering a "trip" of dotterel having a feeding break during a northward migratory journey, though Pendle, a hill clearly visible from Ingleborough, is the one to climb to see dotterel in early May. So confiding is the dotterel that there is time to take in some of the fine points of the plumage – white eye-stripe, white chest band, chestnut underparts and black on the crown and belly.

Swifts have food-hunting jaunts from their nesting areas in local towns and villages. In late autumn, snow buntings, refugees from a northern winter, dance in the air like snowflakes as the wind carries them to the next patch of purple moor-grass, on the seeds of which they are feeding.

Return the same way, taking special care on the stone steps and the boardwalk if they are damp.

Clapham Woods

Approached from Clapham.

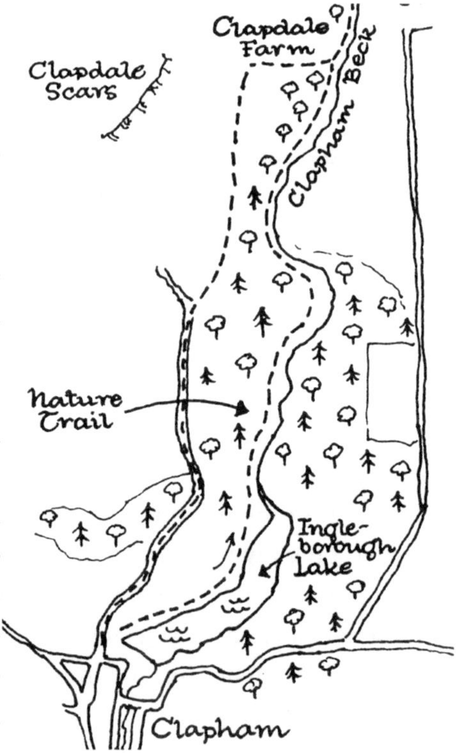

After parking at Clapham, stand on the stone footbridge and look for a dipper and grey wagtail. The collared dove is here, of course, and so are various finches, including greenfinch and goldfinch. Clapham has its nesting swifts and swallows. House martins have been few in number in recent times.

Clapham Woods are owned by Ingleborough Estate, who make a small charge for entry as visitors pass through the woodyard at the head of Clapham village. The valley is Clapdale, well wooded and with a dam holding back the water of Fell Beck as a large but relatively deep lake, unattractive to waterfowl.

The woodland holds a variety of nesting birds - sparrowhawk, woodcock, tawny owl, great spotted woodpecker, various warblers and members of the tit family. The nuthatch has been seen here. Go at anytime of year to see the tree-creeper scurrying up the trunk of a tree and, by its plumage, looking like a little mouse. The relatively long tail is stiffened and is used as a prop as the bird stops to probe with its fine bill into cracks and crannies for food.

The open country round about is the nesting ground of lapwing, curlew, redshank. In winter, there is little more to see than crows and feral pheasants. The beck is fished by a heron.

Ribble Valley

Approached from Long Preston

Below Settle, the Ribble Valley is broad and shallow with the river running deep, between sandy banks, with so many ox-bows it looks like a squiggle on the map. An unusual Enclosure Act of 1799 involved not only the division of the land by walls but the drainage of the lower riverside meadows and pastures and the embanking and control of streams and river. Floodbanks alongside the river do not contain the water after especially heavy rain on the fells or when there is a snowmelt. Lakes appear.

At migration times, the valley holds large numbers of waders. In spring, if a cold snap has checked the course of migration, there might be several thousand lapwings, plus hundreds of curlews and golden plover. Many years ago, in late summer, a huge moulting flock of curlew littered the valley with feathers, lapwings were profuse and several hundred golden plover arrived.

When the valley holds water, in winter or summer, first call at Gallaber, an area of floodwater just north of Hellifield. Those who do

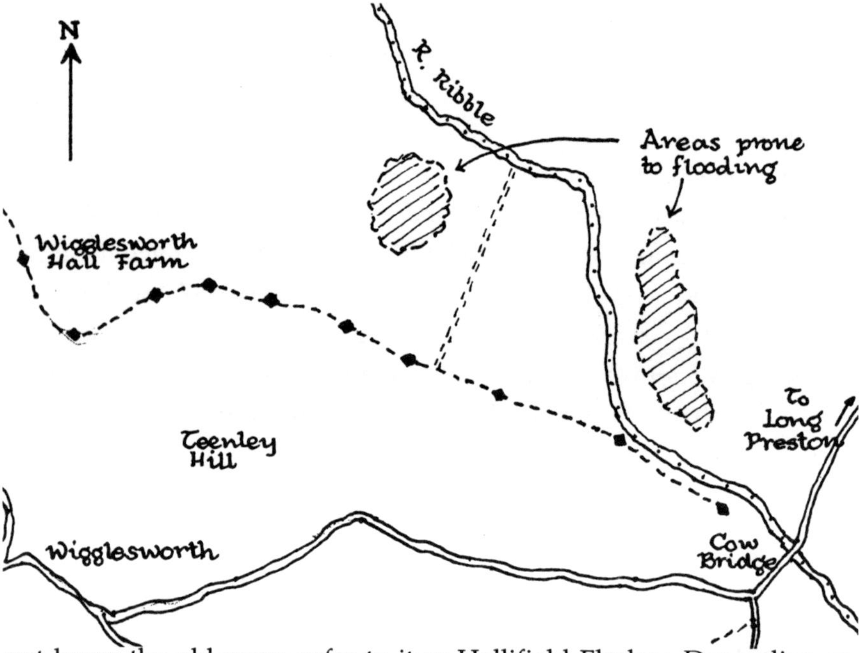

not know the old name refer to it as Hellifield Flashes. Depending on the depth of the water, the area is attractive to ducks or to migrating waders probing in the mud. A road leading to Hellifield station passes close to the flooded area and there is a lay-bye which is also a good vantage point.

Then go via Long Preston, making the first turn left in the village and parking near Cow Bridge. Cross the bridge for a path, part of the Ribble Way, which extends to Wigglesworth Hall and beyond. Here, on a hillock, an extensive view is possible of areas of floodwater. The walk itself, which is easy on the feet, offers the prospect in spring of seeing a variety of waterside birds, including dipper, grey wagtail, oystercatcher, heron, various species of gull and an assortment of waders. Other birds nesting in the valley are mute swan, shelduck, goosander, curlew, lapwing, oystercatcher, snipe, sandpiper and sand martin. In winter, the valley might hold several hundred Canada geese, which have commuted from Stocks reservoir, and also a considerable number of immigrant wigeon.

Malham Tarn

Approached from Settle or Arncliffe.

From Settle, where the A65 is now a by-pass, use the B6479 to Langcliffe. A steep and winding road leads to Cowside Farm and on to Malham Moor. From Arncliffe, turn off the Upper Wharfedale road (B6160) near Kilnsey Crag. The initial stretch from Arncliffe and a descent to Darnbrook Farm are very steep. At the Tarn limited parking is available at the roadside to the north of Tarn Moss. The main parking area is near the outflow of the Tarn to the south.

The National Trust owns Malham Tarn estate and the unmetalled

road serving the House is part of the Pennine Way. From it, north-west of the Tarn, is a bird-watching hide, available to the public. The Tarn, at an elevation of 1,200ft/365m, is situated in classic limestone country, the water being retained by a saucer-shaped depression of impervious Silurian rock. On the western side is Tarn Moss and to the north of the water stands Malham Tarn House, a well-known field centre run by the Field Studies Council. Behind the house are Tarn Woods.

The Tarn is a nesting place for several pairs of great-crested grebe and, occasionally, for the little grebe (also known as the dabchick). Tufted duck, coot and mallard breed at this high-lying tarn and, in spring, the tittering call of the sandpiper is heard as birds arrive for breeding. In autumn and winter, there are occasional sights of whooper swans. Well over 500 coot are recorded in autumn and winter. In autumn, quite large numbers of twite are seen around the Tarn or beside local roads.

In Tarn Woods, nesting species include the redstart, spotted and pied flycatchers, nuthatch, wood warbler, garden warbler and blackcap. Malham Moor is good wheatear country. Red grouse, golden plover and dunlin nest on Fountains Fell, where the natural vegetation has been much improved through good management by the National Trust.

Langstrothdale

From Buckden, at the head of Wharfedale

The road from Buckden to Beckermonds, a hamlet situated where two becks meet to form the Wharfe, is itself a good viewpoint for birdlife in this narrow dale. A low level footpath connects Hubberholme to Yockenthwaite. From Raisgill to the head of the dale, the road is unfenced.

Warm sunny days should be avoided. At such a time, many visitors park their cars and attract sandwich-hungry black-headed gulls.

Winter in Langstrothdale has its special delights, but not for keen bird-watchers, most species departing after the nesting season. The dipper is present except during long dry spells, when reaches of the Wharfe dry out in this limestone country. The grey wagtail nests locally. Sandpipers are active.

Goosanders may be seen. Oystercatchers, curlew and redshank breed in the low fields, especially those which remain traditional pastures or hay meadows. Snipe patronise marshy areas and display in spring. Stands of timber beside the old farmsteads are the nesting place of redstarts.

Strid Wood

Approached from the Cavendish Pavilion

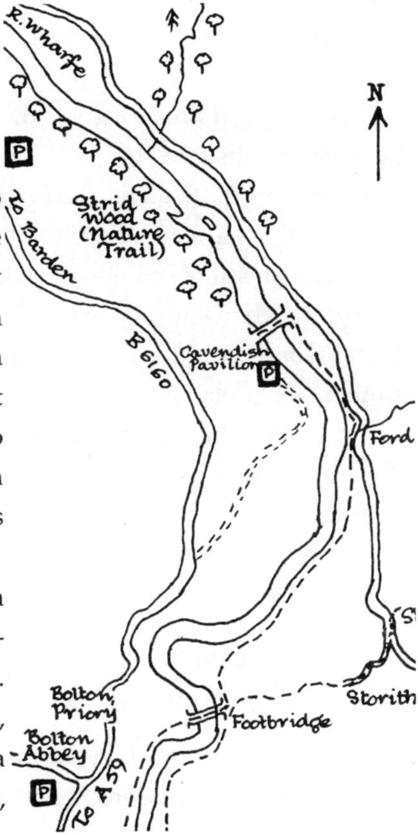

Leave the A59 for Bolton Abbey. Continue through the village to Eastby and Embsay beyond where the road narrows and is spanned by a venerable archway. Shortly an imposing memorial will be seen on the right of the road. Turn right just beyond to follow a private road to Cavendish Pavilion, near which is a riverside car park. A charge is made for access.

An inexpensive leaflet from a small shop gives details of woodland walks, which are colour-coded. Alternately, return to the main road, turn right and motor a little over a mile updale, looking out for a sign,

Strid Wood Car Park, which is on the right, following a path to the river.

There is no better way of spending a pleasant day in the Dales than to walk beside the Wharfe from Bolton Priory to Barden Bridge, returning on the other bank. West of the river, mature woodland fills a narrow gorge in which, at one point, the river goes white with fury as it flows along a natural channel between rocks known as the Strid.

In Strid Wood is a mix of trees of various species and ages, managed with the conservation of wildlife in mind. The trees are mainly oak, beech and sycamore. About 50 bird species nest in this area, and the best time to see them is when April gives way to May and birds are in their nesting places before burgeoning leaves form a thick green curtain.

This is a good area to study the warbler family and to identify it by the various calls and songs. The song of the willow warbler is a series of descending notes. The chiff-chaff calls its name. In the aria of the wood warbler are rapid trills. The blackcap's warble is from a well-concealed position and even more secretive is the garden warbler, the song of which is low-pitched.

The woodland has a goodly number of flycatchers, both pied and spotted, also redstart and both the great spotted and green woodpeckers. In spring, the woodcock flies around its territory in the half light, uttering its "three grunts and a squeak" at intervals. In winter, when the trees are bare and stark, flocks of assorted titmice, in the company of one or two goldcrests and perhaps a tree creeper, keep the avian interest alive. The sparrowhawk frequents the woodland edges.

Grimwith Reservoir

Between Wharfedale and Nidderdale.

Approach Grimwith from either Grassington in Wharfedale or Pateley Bridge in Nidderdale, using the B6265. The entrance is plainly

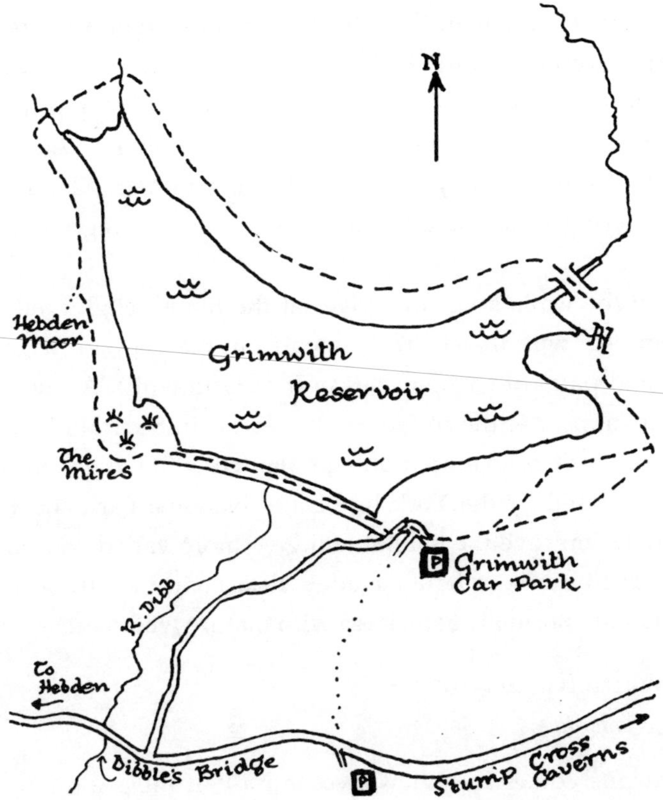

marked on the Greenhow side of Dibbles Bridge, which spans the outflow. A water authority road extends to a car park (and toilet block), with parking available for visitors.

Grimwith, almost 1,000ft/300m above sea level, is in a recess of moorland and has a peripheral path of 4½ miles/7km. The original Bradford was enlarged by the water authority in a scheme which took 10 years, involved the shifting of 3 million tons of material, and was opened in 1985. The peaty moors, which have the usual Pennine mix of ling, various berried shrubs and bracken, are the nesting haunt of red grouse, golden plover, curlew, lapwing, snipe, short-eared owl, meadow pipit and ring ouzel, also whinchat and wheatear.

Allow rather more than two hours for a walk around the reservoir. It is best undertaken anti-clockwise, leaving to the end a stroll (on grass) beside the dam wall, which is wide and mossy, a prime perch for oystercatchers. The ringed plover nests at Grimwith. A large flock of Canada geese is usually to be found grazing on grassland near the dam. Wintering birds include such celebrities as peregrine, buzzard and merlin.

Early in the walk, a visitor arrives at the rebuilt High Laithe cruck barn, complete with thatch. To be seen from the path are wigeon and teal (several pairs of each species nest at Grimwith). A few pairs of sandpipers appear at the fringes of the reservoir. Several plots of land on the shore have been fenced off and planted with indigenous trees in a scheme devised by the Yorkshire Dales National Park and Forestry Authority to improve the habitat and give more varied conditions for wildlife. The birds seen here include redstart and pied flycatcher, two species that are normally associated with mature woodland.

Gouthwaite Reservoir

In Upper Nidderdale.

Gouthwaite comes into view two and a-half miles along the road from Pateley Bridge to the dale head. Car parking is available just beyond Colthouse Farm. A voluntary contribution is invited for the use of the park. Small viewing areas have been provided on the opposite side of the road.

At Gouthwaite, in an area where there was a glacial lake, Bradford Waterworks constructed a compensation reservoir in 1899. Gouthwaite, which has a length of 3 miles/4.8km, is comparatively narrow. In the nesting season, sandpipers are seen and the yellow wagtail is another summer visitor for nesting. Variations in water level usually frustrate any great-crested grebe which attempts to nest.

Ringed plover, both great and little, are occasionally found nesting on the marsh, as does the Canada goose. Passage migrants include greenshank and ruff. The reservoir has considerable appeal in the autumn and winter months, especially when a fall in water level has exposed large areas of silted mud on the northern end. This appeals to waders, whereas diving duck are seen on deeper water. Goldeneye, pochard and tufted duck are quite numerous at times.

Grey geese sometimes sojourn here. Feral birds, including barnacle and lesser snow geese, find the area attractive. Whooper swans, of

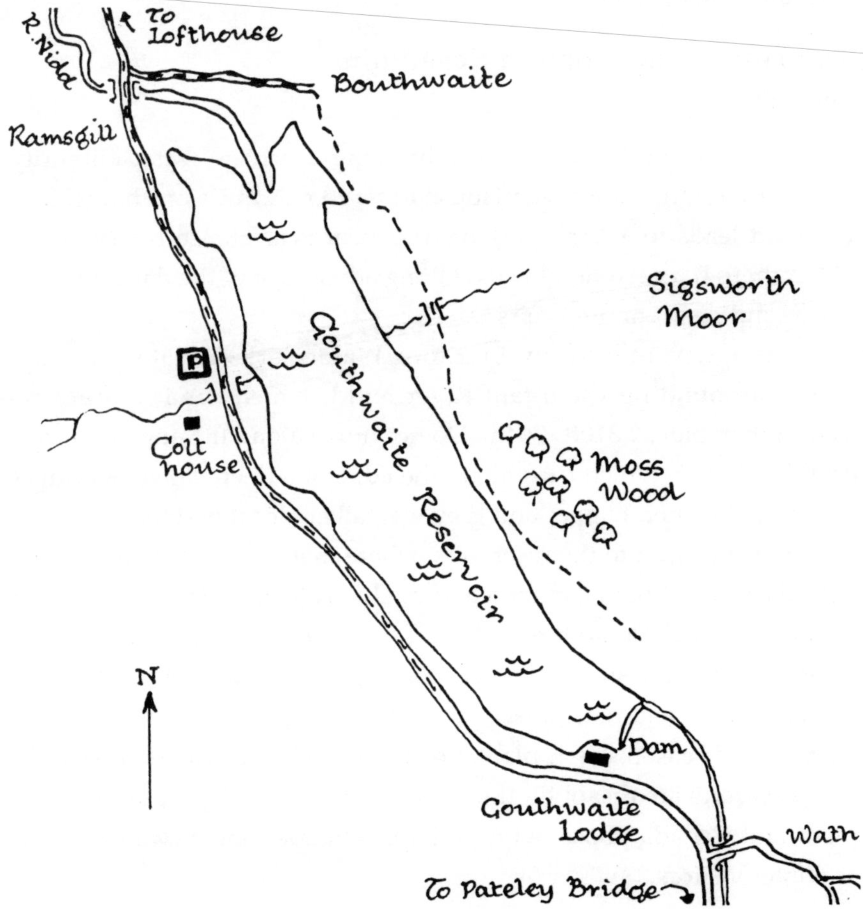

Icelandic origin, are both seen and heard, their bugling calls carrying far on calm winter days.

Knowing bird-watchers, scanning the ridge to the east of Gouthwaite excitedly record wintering birds of prey, sightings including both common and rough-legged buzzard, hen and marsh harrier, sparrowhawk and goshawk, peregrine falcon and merlin. Kites, both red and black, and golden eagle are among the rarities. Gouthwaite has a notable winter gull roost in winter, with black-headed and common gulls much in evidence.

Scar House and Angram Reservoirs

Upper Nidderdale

Just beyond Lofthouse, turn right along a private water authority road with a signpost for Scar House Reservoir. Admission charge: 50p. The road leads to a large parking area near Scar House reservoir, for which there is a peripheral walk, taking advantage of the dams for Scar House and Angram reservoirs.

The dams were built by Bradford Waterworks in late Victorian times, impounding the infant River Nidd, which has its source on Great Whernside, 2,310ft/704m. Do not hurry along the approach road from Lofthouse, which runs along the edge of a deep valley, its ridges tufty with heather. Dipper and grey wagtail are local nesters.

At the approach to the reservoirs, where there are mature trees, look for redstarts and both common and pied flycatchers, also great spotted woodpeckers. The road breaks free of trees and the open ground is the resort of wheatear and whinchat. Waders nesting in the hillside fields include curlew and redshank.

In the off season, larch plantations are used as roosts by buzzards. The reservoirs are disappointing to a bird-watcher. Expect to see sandpiper and Canada goose, with perhaps whooper and Bewick's swans as winter visitors.

Nidderdale Moors

Approach on the zig-zag road climbing the hill from Lofthouse.

The well-managed moorland between Nidderdale and Leighton reservoir can be scanned from an unfenced road, the birds including short-eared owl and buzzard. In springtime, cock grouse are displaying. Meadow pipits descend, trilling. The hidden valley of Colsterdale, which has a length of about 3 miles/4.8km, and is entered between Leighton reservoir and Healey, is celebrated for the number and variety of birds of prey seen in winter.

Semerwater

Approached from Bainbridge, Wensleydale.

This lake of glacial origin, situated in Raydale, is at an elevation of 830ft/250m and is relatively shallow, the maximum depth being 33ft/10m. The lake is notorious for its flash-floods, one of which probably overwhelmed an ancient lakeside settlement and gave rise to a tradition that a beggar man whose calls for food went unheeded cursed the place, which was destroyed by a flood. Sir William Watson wrote a fanciful version of the story as a ballad.

The approach to Semerwater is from Bainbridge (A684), using an unclassified road via Countersett to a parking space at the Carlow Stone, one of several geological erratics standing on a shingly beach. Alternatively, use a narrow road branching from the A684 just east of Bainbridge and terminating at Stalling Busk, from which a footpath leads to the Yorkshire Wildlife Trust's reserve of 53 acres/21ha. A footpath extends along the eastern shoreline.

Water from several small dales converges to form Crooks Beck, which enters Semerwater at the southern end, the outflow being the River Bain, a tributary of the Ure. The Bain is locally thought of as the shortest river in the land, being rather more than 2 miles/3.2km.

In summer, water-skiers use the lake. The noise-tolerant water species are Canada goose, great-crested grebe and coot. Mallards are numerous and it is suspected that the wigeon has nested here.

Nesting in the vicinity of Semerwater are the typical Pennine wading birds – curlew, lapwing, redshank, snipe and oystercatcher. Among the summer visitors to Raydale is the yellow wagtail. Several moorland colonies of black-headed gulls are known and after nesting many converge for a while on the area. Whooper swans are winter visitors. In the relative quietness of winter, grey geese may also appear. Also look out for goldeneye, tufted duck, pochard and teal. The hen harrier has been recorded in the "off" season.

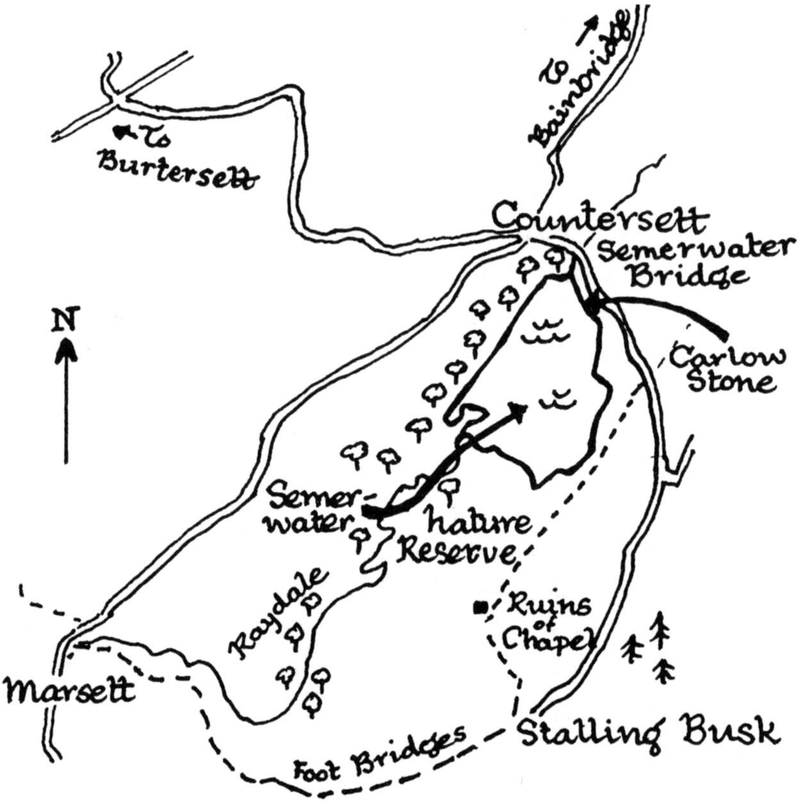

Stocks Reservoir

Approached from Slaidburn, Tosside or Clapham

The reservoir, which lies at 700ft/220m, covers 344 acres/140 hectares in the upper valley of the Hodder. This is the principal water-course of Bowland and the main tributary of the Ribble. A car park on the eastern side is ideal for bird-watchers, a track leading to a hide overlooking the water. A good view of an island is to be had from a causeway flanked by walls which is to be found between an isolated church and the aforementioned car park.

The island is the nesting place of about 500 pairs of black-headed gulls, also Canada geese. Several hundred Canada geese are associated with this area, some of them nesting on nearby moorland. There is quite often a group of cormorants on the island. Greylag also nest in the area, along with teal and tufted duck.

In winter, a large gull roost is recorded. Bird visitors include whooper swan, wigeon, goldeneye and pochard. The hen harrier is a "regular rarity". As an important place on a trans-Pennine migration route, Stocks sometimes plays host to shelduck. The osprey occurs on migration.

In Gisburn Forest, on the gathering grounds to the east, are sparrowhawk, goshawk, long-eared, short-eared tawny owl and siskin.

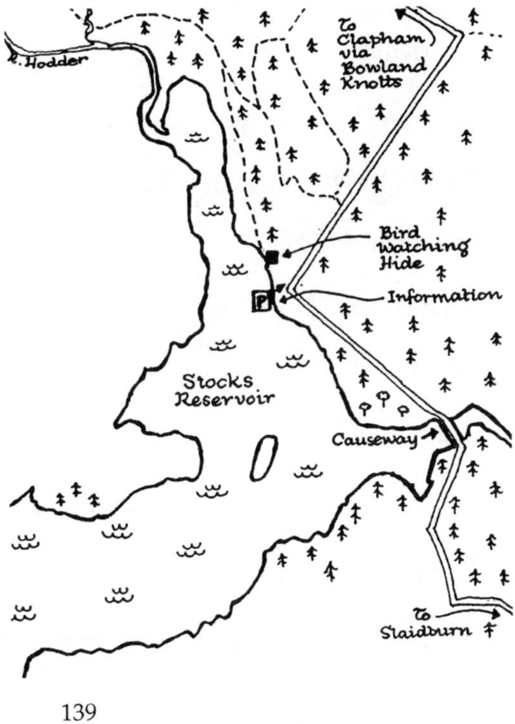

A PERSONAL CHECK LIST

This list is not exhaustive, so space is left at the end for birds not listed.

NAME	WHERE SEEN	DATE
Great Crested Grebe		
Slavonian Grebe		
Little Grebe		
Cormorant		
Grey Heron		
Mute Swan		
Whooper Swan		
Bewick's Swan		
Greylag Goose		
Pink-footed Goose		
Canada Goose		
Shelduck		
Mallard		
Gadwall		

NAME	WHERE SEEN	DATE
Wigeon		
Pintail		
Teal		
Pochard		
Tufted Duck		
Goldeneye		
Red-breasted Merganser		
Goosander		
Honey Buzzard		
Common Buzzard		
Rough-legged Buzzard		
Goshawk		
Sparrow Hawk		
Hen Harrier		
Kestrel		
Merlin		
Peregrine		
Pheasant		
Partridge		

NAME	WHERE SEEN	DATE
Moorhen		
Coot		
Oystercatcher		
Ringed Plover		
Dotterel		
Golden Plover		
Lapwing		
Dunlin		
Snipe		
Woodcock		
Curlew		
Redshank		
Greenshank		
Common Sandpiper		
Black-headed Gull		
Common Gull		
Great Black-backed Gull		
Lesser Black-backed Gull		
Herring Gull		

NAME	WHERE SEEN	DATE
Collared Dove		
Cuckoo		
Stock Dove		
Woodpigeon		
Barn Owl		
Little Owl		
Tawny Owl		
Long-eared Owl		
Short-eared Owl		
Nightjar		
Kingfisher		
Green Woodpecker		
Great Spotted Woodpecker		
Lesser Spotted Woodpecker		
Skylark		
Swift		
Sand Martin		
Swallow		
House Martin		

NAME	WHERE SEEN	DATE
Meadow Pipit		
Tree Pipit		
Yellow Wagtail		
Grey Wagtail		
Pied Wagtail		
Waxwing		
Dipper		
Wren		
Dunnock		
Robin		
Redstart		
Whinchat		
Stonechat		
Wheatear		
Ring Ouzel		
Blackbird		
Redwing		
Fieldfare		
Song Thrush		

NAME	WHERE SEEN	DATE
Mistle Thrush		
Whitethroat		
Garden Warbler		
Blackcap		
Wood Warbler		
Chiff Chaff		
Willow Warbler		
Goldcrest		
Spotted Flycatcher		
Pied Flycatcher		
Long-tailed Tit		
Blue Tit		
Great Tit		
Marsh Tit		
Coal Tit		
Nuthatch		
Tree Creeper		
Jay		
Magpie		

NAME	WHERE SEEN	DATE
Jackdaw		
Rook		
Carrion Crow		
Raven		
Starling		
House Sparrow		
Tree Sparrow		
Chaffinch		
Brambling		
Goldfinch		
Greenfinch		
Siskin		
Linnet		
Twite		
Redpoll		
Snow Bunting		
Reed Bunting		
Yellow Hammer		

Other species seen –

NAME	WHERE SEEN	DATE

BIBLIOGRAPHY

Appleyard, Ian – Ring Ouzels of the Yorkshire Dales (1994)
Dickens, R F, and Mitchell, W R – Birdwatching in Yorkshire (1977)
Gilbert, H A, and Arthur Brook – Secrets of Bird Life (1924)
Mather, John R – Where to Watch Birds in Yorkshire (2nd ed., 1998)
Nelson, T H – The Birds of Yorkshire, two volumes (1907)
Ratcliffe, Derek – Bird Life of Mountain and Upland

Whooper Swans